Basic
Korean
for Travelers

TALK! TALK!
Basic Korean
for Travelers

초판 1쇄 발행 2024년 4월 30일

지은이 시원스쿨어학연구소
펴낸곳 (주)에스제이더블유인터내셔널
펴낸이 양홍걸 이시원

홈페이지 korean.siwonschool.com
주소 서울시 영등포구 영신로 166 시원스쿨
교재 구입 문의 02)2014-8151
고객센터 02)6409-0878

ISBN 979-11-6150-844-3 13700
Number 1-587271-26260400-08

TALK! TALK!

Basic Korean
for Travelers

✈ Preface

"Travel Korean" was created with the following idea in mind.

The Korean language may seem like an easy language to learn even with just a basic understanding of its principles. However, communicating naturally in Korean can take anywhere from two months to an entire year.

If our book, "Travel Korean," were to include a comprehensive list of all the principles of the Korean language, it would need to be three times thicker than its current size, which would not be convenient to carry around as a book.

If you are planning a trip to Korea for one to three months, you will need a book that you can find information quickly from. It should provide you with words and phrases that you can utilize in the moment, in any situation.

This book is the first of its kind in Korea, using situations, then words, then sentences, as the design structure. It allows you to recall words related to specific situations and find readily usable sentences. The sole purpose of this book is to help you find Korean terms and speak in Korean quickly.

Contents

📖 vocabulary index

C

D

G

H

I

J

M

Y

What is Hangeul?

"Hangeul" refers to the Korean alphabet, and it was created by King Sejong in the 15th century. Before the creation of Hangeul, Korean people used a writing system that borrowed Chinese characters, but it was difficult for many to express their thoughts. To solve this problem, King Sejong created Hangeul, a unique system of Korean letters that everyone could learn easily.

Special Characteristics of the Korean Language

1 There is no accent.

2 Hangeul is phonetic.

3 There are 14 consonants and 10 vowels.

4 There are honorific expressions.

The Structure of Korean Syllables

Korean syllables function as building blocks or bricks. Each brick fits at least two Hangeul letters. The letter combinations must include both consonants and vowels. There are 3 kinds of letter combinations: horizonal, vertical, and mixed.Korean syllables function as building blocks or bricks. Each brick fits at least two Hangeul letters. The letter combinations must include both consonants and vowels. There are 3 kinds of letter combinations: horizonal, vertical, and mixed.

Here are a few examples

Horizontal Combinations 다, 달, 닭
Vertical Combinations 도, 돌, 돐
Mixed Combinations 되, 됨, 됇

✦ 자음 (초성 모음 앞)

한글	로마자	한글	로마자
ㄱ	g	ㅉ	jj
ㄲ	kk	ㅊ	ch
ㅋ	k	ㅅ	s
ㄷ	d	ㅆ	ss
ㄸ	tt	ㅎ	h
ㅌ	t	ㄴ	n
ㅂ	b	ㅁ	m
ㅃ	pp	ㅇ	(소리 없음. 모음에 따라)
ㅍ	p	ㄹ	r
ㅈ	j		

✦ 자음 (받침)

받침		로마자
ㄱ	ㄲ, ㅋ	k
ㄴ		n
ㄷ	ㅌ, ㅅ, ㅆ, ㅈ, ㅊ	t
ㄹ		l
ㅁ		m
ㅂ	ㅍ	p
ㅇ		ng

✤ 모음

한글	로마자	한글	로마자
ㅏ	a	ㅑ	ya
ㅓ	eo	ㅕ	yeo
ㅗ	o	ㅛ	yo
ㅜ	u	ㅠ	yu
ㅡ	eu	ㅒ	yae
ㅣ	i	ㅖ	ye
ㅐ	ae	ㅘ	wa
ㅔ	e	ㅙ	wae
ㅚ	oe	ㅝ	wo
ㅟ	wi	ㅞ	we
		ㅢ	ui

On an airplane

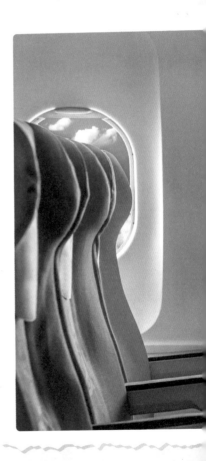

Frequently used words on an airplane

01 seat
jwa-seok
좌석

02 this
i-geo
이거

03 seat belt
an-jeon-bel-teu
안전벨트

04 restroom
hwa-jang-sil
화장실

05 toilet
byeon-gi
변기

06 screen
hwa-myeon
화면

07 light
bul
불

08 napkin
hyu-ji
휴지

09 blanket
dam-yo
담요

10 headset
he-deu-pon
헤드폰

11	remote control	ri-mo-keon 리모컨
12	newspaper	sin-mun 신문
13	drink	ma-sil geot 마실 것
14	snack	gan-sik-geo-ri 간식거리
15	meal	sik-sa 식사
16	eye patch	an-dae 안대
17	pillow	be-gae 베개
18	slippers	seul-li-peo 슬리퍼
19	entry card	ip-guk-sin-go-seo 입국신고서

20 **customs form**

se-gwan-sin-go-seo
세관신고서

21 **pen**

pen
펜

22 **tax-free goods**

gi-nae myeon-se-pum
기내 면세품

Find and speak phrases quickly!

seat   jwa-seok
좌석

· This is my seat.   **je ja-ri-in-de-yo**
제 자리인데요.

· Where is my seat?   **je ja-ri eo-din-ga-yo?**
제 자리 어딘가요?

· Don't kick my seat.   **je ja-ri cha-ji ma-se-yo**
제 자리 차지 마세요.

this   i-geo
이거

· What is this?   **i-geo mwo-ye-yo?**
이거 뭐예요?

· Get me this.   **i-geo ga-jyeo-da-ju-se-yo**
이거 가져다주세요.

· This doesn't work.   **i-geo an dwae-yo**
이거 안 돼요.

· Take this away.   **i-geo chi-wo ju-se-yo**
이거 치워 주세요.

· Get me a different one.   **i-geo ba-kkwo ju-se-yo**
이거 바꿔 주세요.

· I will go with this one. **i-geo-ro hal-ge-yo**
이거로 할게요.

seat belt **an-jeon-bel-teu**
안전벨트

· Fasten your seat belt. **an-jeon-bel-teu-reul mae-se-yo**
안전벨트를 매세요.

· I can't find my seat belt. **je an-jeon-bel-teu-reul mot chat-ge-sseo-yo**
제 안전벨트를 못 찾겠어요.

· My seat belt is loose. **je an-jeon-bel-teu-ga heol-leong-hae-yo**
제 안전벨트가 헐렁해요.

· My seat belt is too tight. **je an-jeon-bel-teu-ga neo-mu ta-i-teu-hae-yo**
제 안전벨트가 너무 타이트해요.

restroom hwa-jang-sil
화장실

· The restroom is dirty.
hwa-jang-si-ri deo-reo-wo-yo
화장실이 더러워요.

· The restroom is not clean.
hwa-jang-sil cheong-so-ga an doe-eo-sseo-yo
화장실 청소가 안 되었어요.

· Is someone in the restroom?
nu-ga hwa-jang-si-re in-na-yo?
누가 화장실에 있나요?

· Is this the line for the restroom?
i-geo hwa-jang-sil ju-rin-ga-yo?
이거 화장실 줄인가요?

toilet byeon-gi
변기

· The toilet got clogged.
byeon-gi-ga ma-kyeo-sseo-yo
변기가 막혔어요.

screen

hwa-myeon
화면

· Could you take a look at my screen?

je hwa-myeon han-beon bwa ju-sil-lae-yo?
제 화면 한번 봐 주실래요?

· My screen is not working.

hwa-myeo-ni an na-wa-yo
화면이 안 나와요.

· My screen has frozen.

hwa-myeo-ni meom-chwo-sseo-yo
화면이 멈췄어요.

· My screen is too bright.

hwa-myeo-ni neo-mu bal-ga-yo
화면이 너무 밝아요.

light

bul
불

· How do I turn on the light?

bul eo-tteo-ke kyeo-yo?
불 어떻게 켜요?

· The light is too bright.

bu-ri neo-mu bal-ga-yo
불이 너무 밝아요.

· Please turn off the light.

bul jom kkeo ju-se-yo
불 좀 꺼 주세요.

napkin

hyu-ji
휴지

· Give me some napkins.

naep-kin jom ju-se-yo
냅킨 좀 주세요.

· Give me some more napkins.

naep-kin jom deo ju-se-yo
냅킨 좀 더 주세요.

blanket

dam-yo
담요

· I got no blanket.

jeo dam-yo-eop-seo-yo
저 담요 없어요.

· Get me a blanket.

dam-yo ga-jyeo-da ju-se-yo
담요 가져다주세요.

· Could you get me another blanket?

jeo dam-yo ha-na-man deo ju-se-yo
저 담요 하나만 더 주세요.

headset

he-deu-pon

헤드폰

· Get me the headset.

he-deu-pon ga-jyeo-da ju-se-yo

헤드폰 가져다주세요.

· My headset is not working.

he-deu-po-ni an doe-neun-de-yo

헤드폰이 안 되는데요.

· (Showing the jack) Where does this go?

eo-di-da kko-ja-yo?

(잭을 보여주며) 어디다 꽂아요?

· Can I keep it?

jeo i-geo ga-jyeo-do dwae-yo?

저 이거 가져도 돼요?

remote control

ri-mo-keon

리모컨

· Get me a remote control.

ri-mo-keon ga-jyeo-da ju-se-yo

리모컨 좀 가져다주세요.

· My remote control is not working.

ri-mo-keo-ni an doe-neun-de-yo

리모컨이 안 되는데요.

· Get me another remote control.

ri-mo-keon da-reun geol-lo gat-da ju-se-yo
리모컨 다른 걸로 갖다 주세요.

newspaper sin-mun
신문

· Get me a newspaper.

sin-mun jom gat-da ju-se-yo
신문 좀 갖다 주세요.

· Do you have sports newspapers?

seu-po-cheu sin-mun i-sseo-yo?
스포츠 신문 있어요?

drink ma-sil geot
마실 것

· Get me something to drink.

ma-sil geo jom ju-se-yo
마실 거 좀 주세요.

· Get me some water.

mul jom ju-se-yo
물 좀 주세요.

· Get me some orange juice.

o-ren-ji ju-seu jom ju-se-yo
오렌지 주스 좀 주세요.

· Get me some Coke.

kol-la jom ju-se-yo
콜라 좀 주세요.

· Get me some Sprite.

sa-i-da jom ju-se-yo
사이다 좀 주세요.

· Get me some green tea.

nok-cha jom ju-se-yo
녹차 좀 주세요.

· Get me some coffee.

keo-pi jom ju-se-yo
커피 좀 주세요.

· Get me some beer.

maek-ju jom ju-se-yo
맥주 좀 주세요.

· Get me some wine.

wa-in jom ju-se-yo
와인 좀 주세요.

snack

gan-sik-geo-ri
간식거리

· You got some snacks?

gan-sik geo-ri jom in-na-yo?
간식 거리 좀 있나요?

· Get me some more peanuts.

ttang-kong jom deo ju-se-yo
땅콩 좀 더 주세요.

50

· Get me some more pretzels.	**peu-re-jeul jom deo ju-se-yo** 프레즐 좀 더 주세요.
· Get me some cookies.	**ku-ki jom ju-se-yo** 쿠키 좀 주세요.

meal

sik-sa
식사

· When is the meal?	**sik-sa-ga eon-je-in-ga-yo?** 식사가 언제인가요?
· What do you have for the meal?	**sik-sa-ga mwo-in-ga-yo?** 식사가 뭐인가요?
· I'll have my meal later.	**sik-sa na-jung-e hal-ge-yo** 식사 나중에 할게요.
· I'll have my meal now.	**ji-geum jeo sik-sa hal-ge-yo** 지금 저 식사할게요.

eyepatch an-dae

안대

· Do you have an eyepatch?

an-dae i-sseo-yo?

안대 있어요?

· This eyepatch isn't comfy.

i an-dae bul-pyeon-hae-yo

이 안대 불편해요.

· Get me another eyepatch.

da-reun an-dae gat-da ju-se-yo

다른 안대 갖다 주세요.

pillow be-gae

베개

· Do you have a pillow?

be-gae i-sseo-yo?

베개 있어요?

· This pillow isn't comfy.

i be-gae bul-pyeon-hae-yo

이 베개 불편해요.

· Get me another pillow.

da-reun be-gae gat-da ju-seyo
다른 베개 갖다 주세요.

slippers

seul-li-peo
슬리퍼

· Do you have slippers?

seul-li-peo i-sseo-yo?
슬리퍼 있어요?

· These slippers are not comfy.

i seul-li-peo bul-pyeon-hae-yo
이 슬리퍼 불편해요.

entry card

ip-guk-sin-go-seo
입국신고서

· Help me with this entry card.

ip-guk-sin-go-seo jak-seong jom do-wa-jwo-yo
입국신고서 작성 좀 도와줘요.

· Please get me one more entry card.

ip-guk-sin-go-seo han jang deo jwo-yo
입국신고서 한 장 더 줘요.

customs form se-gwan-sin-go-seo
세관신고서

· Help me with this customs form.

se-gwan-sin-go-seo jak-seong jom do-wa-jwo-yo
세관신고서 작성 좀 도와줘요.

· Please get me one more customs form.

se-gwan-sin-go-seo han jang deo jwo-yo
세관신고서 한 장 더 줘요.

pen pen
펜

· Can I borrow a pen?

pen jom bil-lyeo-ju-si-ge-sseo-yo?
펜 좀 빌려 주시겠어요?

· This pen doesn't work.

i pen an na-wa-yo
이 펜 안 나와요.

· Get me another pen.

da-reun pen-eu-ro ju-se-yo
다른 펜으로 주세요.

tax-free goods

gi-nae myeon-se-pum

기내 면세품

· Show me some tax-free goods.

gi-nae myeon-se-pum jom bo-yeo jwo-yo

기내 면세품 좀 보여줘요.

· Do you take credit cards?

sin-yong-ka-deu doe-na-yo?

신용카드 되나요?

Emergency situation

headache
du-tong
두통

cold
eu-seu-reu-seul
으슬으슬

stomachache
bok-tong
복통

sick
a-pa-yo
아파요

dizzy
eo-ji-reo-um
어지러움

airsick
bi-haeng-gi meol-mi
비행기 멀미

Find and speak phrases quickly!

· I think I have a headache.

jeo du-tong in-neun geot ga-ta-yo
저 두통 있는 것 같아요.

· Get me some aspirin.

du-tong-nyak jom ju-se-yo
두통약 좀 주세요.

· I think I have a stomachache.

jeo bok-tong in-neun geot ga-ta-yo
저 복통 있는 것 같아요.

· I feel dizzy.

jeo eo-ji-reo-wo-yo
저 어지러워요.

· I feel cold.

jeo eu-seu-reu-seul-hae-yo
저 으슬으슬해요.

· I feel sick.

jeo a-pa-yo
저 아파요.

· I feel airsick.

jeo meol-mi-na-yo
저 멀미나요.

memo

In-flight Meals, Korean Airlines

Korean Air and Asiana Airlines provide a variety of special in-flight meals upon request for customers who cannot have regular meals due to health problems, allergies to certain foods, religion, or age. There are various options, including meals for children, vegetarian or vegan guests, passengers observing religious diets, and those with other special dietary requirements.

You can check each airline's in-flight meal options on the following websites:

Korean Air https://www.koreanair.com/kr/en/in-flight/onboard-service/dining/economy

Asiana Airlines https://flyasiana.com/C/GB/EN/contents/class-information

For Korean Air, you need to apply for special in-flight meals on their website or contact their service center.

In the case of Asiana Airlines, you can order special in-flight meals by calling the relevant branch number.

At the airport

Frequently used words at the airport

01	transit	hwan-seung 환승
02	gate	ge-i-teu 게이트
03	boarding	tap-seung 탑승
04	delay	yeon-chak 연착
05	next flight	da-eum bi-haeng-pyeon 다음 비행편
06	wait	dae-gi 대기
07	lounge	dae-gi jang-so 대기 장소
08	restaurant	re-seu-to-rang 레스토랑
09	duty-free shop	myeon-se-jeom 면세점
10	restroom	hwa-jang-sil 화장실

11	immigration	chu-rip-guk-gwal-li-so 출입국관리소
12	international	oe-gu-gin 외국인
13	interpreter	tong-yeok-sa 통역사
14	fingerprint	ji-mun 지문
15	return ticket	wang-bok ti-ket 왕복 티켓
16	I'm here on	yeo-gi wae wan-nya-myeon-yo 여기 왜 왔냐면요
17	I'm staying at	yeo-gi mu-geul geo-ye-yo 여기 묵을 거예요
18	I'm here for	(period) dong-an i-sseul geo-ye-yo (period) 동안 있을 거예요.

19	baggage claim	su-ha-mul chan-neun got 수하물 찾는 곳
20	trolley	ka-teu 카트
21	missing	bun-sil 분실
22	mine	je geo-ye-yo 제 거예요
23	declare	sin-go 신고
24	gift	seon-mul 선물
25	exit	chul-gu 출구
26	information center	yeo-haeng-an-nae-so 여행안내소
27	money exchange	hwan-jeon 환전

Find and speak phrases quickly!

---

transit

hwan-seung
환승

· I'm a transit passenger.

jeo hwan-seung seung-gaek-in-de-yo
저 환승 승객인데요.

· Is there a transit lounge?

hwan-seung ra-un-ji in-na-yo?
환승 라운지 있나요?

· I'm a transit passenger to Incheon.

gyeong-yu-hae-seo in-cheon-eu-ro ga-yo
경유해서 인천으로 가요.

---

gate ⊞

ge-i-teu
게이트

· I can't find my gate.

je ge-i-teu-reul mot chat-ge-sseo-yo
제 게이트를 못 찾겠어요.

· Where is gate number two?

i-beon ge-i-teu-neun eo-di-e i-sseo-yo?
2번 게이트는 어디에 있어요?

66

boarding

tap-seung
탑승

· When does the boarding start?

tap-seung eon-je hae-yo?
탑승 언제 해요?

· How long do I need to wait to board?

tap-seung-ha-ryeo-myeon eol-ma-na gi-da-reo-yo?
탑승하려면 얼마나 기다려요?

delay

yeon-chak
연착

· Is my flight delayed?

je bi-haeng-gi yeon-chak-dwae-sseo-yo?
제 비행기 연착됐어요?

· Why is my flight delayed?

wae yeon-chak-dwae-sseo-yo?
왜 연착됐어요?

· How long do I have to wait?

eon-je-kka-ji gi-da-ryeo-yo?
언제까지 기다려요?

next flight

da-eum bi-haeng-
pyeon
다음 비행편

· When is the next flight?

da-eum bi-haeng-gi-neun geu-reom eon-je chul-bal-hae-yo?
다음 비행기는 그럼 언제 출발해요?

· Which airline is the next flight?

da-eum bi-haeng-pyeo-neun eo-tteon hang-gong-sa-ye-yo?
다음 비행편은 어떤 항공사예요?

· How much is the next flight?

da-eum bi-haeng-pyeo-neun eol-ma-ye-yo?
다음 비행편은 얼마예요?

· I waited for so long. Get me an upgrade.

o-rae gi-da-ryeo-sseu-ni-kka jwa-seok eop-geu-re-i-deu-hae jwo-yo
오래 기다렸으니까 좌석 업그레이드해 줘요.

---

wait

dae-gi
대기

· How long do I wait?

eol-ma-na dae-gi-hae-yo?
얼마나 대기해요?

· Where do I wait?　**eo-di-seo dae-gi-hae-yo?**
어디서 대기해요?

· Can I go outside while waiting?　**dae-gi-ha-neun dong-an na-gal su-i-sseo-yo?**
대기하는 동안 나갈 수 있어요?

lounge 　dae-gi-jang-so
대기 장소

· Where is the waiting lounge?　**dae-gi-jang-so eo-di-ye-yo?**
대기 장소 어디예요?

· Where is the business lounge?　**bi-jeu-ni-seu ra-un-ji eo-di-ye-yo?**
비즈니스 라운지 어디예요?

restaurant 　re-seu-to-rang
레스토랑

· Where is the restaurant?　**re-seu-to-rang eo-di-ye-yo?**
레스토랑 어디예요?

Where is the coffee shop?	**keo-pi-syop eo-di i-sseo-yo?**
	커피숍 어디 있어요?
Does it take long?	**o-rae geol-lyeo-yo?**
	오래 걸려요?

duty-free shop myeon-se-jeom
면세점

Where are the duty-free shops?	**myeon-se-jeom eo-di-ye-yo?**
	면세점 어디예요?
Is the duty-free shop far from here?	**myeon-se-jeom meo-reo-yo?**
	면세점 멀어요?
Where are the cosmetics?	**hwa-jang-pum eo-di i-sseo-yo?**
	화장품 어디 있어요?
This is a gift.	**seon-mul-hal geo-ye-yo**
	선물할 거예요.

restroom hwa-jang-sil
화장실

· Where is the
restroom?

hwa-jang-sil eo-di i-sseo-yo?
화장실 어디 있어요?

· Is the restroom
outside?

hwa-jang-si-reun ba-kkeu-ro na-ga-ya in-na-yo?
화장실은 밖으로 나가야 있나요?

· Is there a restroom
inside the lounge?

hwa-jang-sil ra-un-ji an-e-neun eop-seo-yo?
화장실 라운지 안에는 없어요?

immigration chu-rip-guk-gwal-li-so
출입국관리소

· Where is the
immigration?

chu-rip-guk-gwal-li-so eo-di-ro ga-yo?
출입국관리소 어디로 가요?

· Where is the
immigration?

ip-guk-sim-sa-dae eo-di-ro ga-yo?
입국심사대 어디로 가요?

international oe-gu-gin
외국인

· Is this a line for internationals?	**i-ge oe-gu-gin ju-rin-ga-yo?** 이게 외국인 줄인가요?
· Is this a line for foreigners?	**i-ge oe-gu-gin ju-rin-ga-yo?** 이게 외국인 줄인가요?

interpreter tong-yeok-sa
통역사

· Can you get me an interpreter?	**tong-yeok-sa bul-leo ju-se-yo** 통역사 불러 주세요.
· I don't understand.	**mot a-ra deut-ge-sseo-yo** 못 알아듣겠어요.
· Can you speak slowly?	**cheon-cheon-hi mal-sseum-hae ju-se-yo** 천천히 말씀해 주세요.

- One more time, please.

da-si han-beon mal-sseum-hae ju-se-yo

다시 한번 말씀해 주세요.

fingerprint

ji-mun

지문

- Put your fingerprint here.

ji-mun yeo-gi-da gat-da dae-se-yo

지문 여기다 갖다 대세요.

- My right hand?

o-reun-jjok son-i-yo?

오른쪽 손이요?

- My left hand?

oen-jjok son-i-yo?

왼쪽 손이요?

return ticket

wang-bok ti-ket

왕복 티켓

- Show me your return ticket.

wang-bok ti-ket bo-yeo ju-se-yo

왕복 티켓 보여 주세요.

- Do you have your return ticket?

wang-bok ti-ket i-sseu-se-yo?

왕복 티켓 있으세요?

Yes. Here is my return ticket.	**ne, yeo-gi je wang-bok ti-ke-si-yo** 네, 여기 제 왕복 티켓이요.

I'm here on 🥜?

yeo-gi wae wan-nya-myeon-yo
여기 왜 왔냐면요.

· I'm here on a vacation.	**hyu-ga bo-nae-reo wa-sseo-yo** 휴가 보내러 왔어요.
· I'm here on a business trip.	**chul-jang ttae-mu-ne wa-sseo-yo** 출장 때문에 왔어요.
· I'm here for sightseeing.	**gwan-gwang-ha-reo wa-sseo-yo** 관광하러 왔어요.

I'm staying at yeo-gi mu-geul geo-ye-yo

여기 묵을 거예요.

· I'm staying at a hotel.

ho-tel-e mu-geul geo-ye-yo

호텔에 묵을 거예요.

· I'm staying at a guest house.

ge-seu-teu-ha-u-seu-e mu-geul geo-ye-yo

게스트하우스에 묵을 거예요.

· I'm staying at my relatives.

chin-cheok ji-be mu-geul geo-ye-yo

친척 집에 묵을 거예요.

I'm here for (period) dong-an i-sseul geo-ye-yo

(period) 동안 있을 거예요.

· I'm here for three days.

sam-il dong-an i-sseul geo-ye-yo

3일 동안 있을 거예요.

· I'm here for a week.

il-ju-il dong-an i-sseul geo-ye-yo

1주일 동안 있을 거예요.

· I'm here for two weeks.
i-ju-il dong-an i-sseul geo-ye-yo
2주일 동안 있을 거예요.

· I'm here for a month.
han dal dong-an i-sseul geo-ye-yo
한 달 동안 있을 거예요.

baggage claim
su-ha-mul chan-neun got
수하물 찾는 곳

· Where do I find my baggage?
su-ha-mul eo-di-seo cha-ja-yo?
수하물 어디서 찾아요?

· Where is the baggage claim?
su-ha-mul chan-neun go-si eo-di-ye-yo?
수하물 찾는 곳이 어디예요?

trolley
ka-teu
카트

· Where is the trolley?
ka-teu eo-di-sseo-yo?
카트 어딨어요?

· Is a trolley free?	**ka-teu gong-jja-ye-yo?**
	카트 공짜예요?
· There is no trolley.	**ka-teu-ga eom-neun-de-yo**
	카트가 없는데요.

missing bun-sil
분실

· My baggage is missing.	**je ji-mi eom-neun-de-yo**
	제 짐이 없는데요.
· My baggage hasn't come out yet.	**je ji-mi an na-wa-sseo-yo**
	제 짐이 안 나왔어요.
· I think I've lost my baggage.	**je ji-meul bun-sil-haen-na-bwa-yo**
	제 짐을 분실했나봐요.

mine je geo-ye-yo
제 거예요.

· This bag is mine.	**i ga-bang je geo-ye-yo**
	이 가방 제 거예요.
· This trolley is mine.	**i ka-teu jeo geo-ye-yo**
	이 카트 제 거예요.

declare

sin-go
신고

· I have nothing to declare.

sin-go-hal mul-geon eop-seo-yo
신고할 물건 없어요.

· I have something to declare.

sin-go-hal mul-geon i-sseo-yo
신고할 물건 있어요.

· Where do I go to declare?

sin-go-ha-ryeo-myeon eo-di-ro ga-jyo?
신고하려면 어디로 가죠?

gift

seon-mul
선물

· These are the gifts.

i-geon seon-mul-hal geo-ye-yo
이건 선물할 거예요.

· This is what I've got as a gift.

i-geon seon-mul ba-deun geo-ye-yo
이건 선물 받은 거예요.

· I bought this as a gift.

seon-mul-lo san geo-ye-yo
선물로 산 거예요.

exit

chul-gu
출구

· Where is the exit?

chul-gu eo-di-ye-yo?
출구 어디예요?

· Which way is the exit?

chul-gu-neun eo-neu jjo-gi-e-yo?
출구는 어느 쪽이에요?

· I can't find the exit.

chul-gu-reul mot chat-ge-sseo-yo
출구를 못 찾겠어요.

information center

yeo-haeng an-nae-so
여행안내소

· Where is the information center?

yeo-haeng-an-nae-so eo-di-ye-yo?
여행안내소 어디예요?

· Please give me a map.

ji-do jom ju-se-yo
지도 좀 주세요.

money exchange

hwan-jeon
환전

· Where is the money exchange?

hwan-jeon-ha-neun de eo-di-ye-yo?
환전하는 데 어디예요?

· I'd like to exchange money.

hwan-jeon-ha-ryeo-go ha-neun-de-yo
환전하려고 하는데요.

· Small bills, please.

jan-do-neu-ro ju-se-yo
잔돈으로 주세요.

taxi

taek-si
택시

· Where do I get a taxi?

taek-si eo-di-seo tal su i-sseo-yo?
택시 어디서 탈 수 있어요?

· Is taking a taxi
expensive?

taek-si ta-myeon bi-ssan-ga-yo?
택시 타면 비싼가요?

· I'm going downtown
by taxi.

taek-si ta-go si-nae ga-ryeo-go-yo
택시 타고 시내 가려고요.

· What else can I take?

taek-si dae-sin mwo tal su i-sseo-yo?
택시 대신 뭐 탈 수 있어요?

---

shuttle bus syeo-teul beo-seu
셔틀버스

· Where can I get a
shuttle bus?

syeo-teul-beo-seu eo-di-seo ta-yo?
셔틀버스 어디서 타요?

· What time does the
shuttle bus leave?

syeo-teul-beo-seu myeot si-e chul-bal-hae-yo?
셔틀버스 몇 시에 출발해요?

· Does this shuttle bus
go downtown?

i syeo-teul beo-seu si-nae ga-yo?
이 셔틀 버스 시내 가요?

· How much is the shuttle bus?

syeo-teul-beo-seu eol-ma-ye-yo?

셔틀버스 얼마예요?

the nearest *je-il ga-kka-un*

제일 가까운

· Where is the nearest hotel?

ga-kkaun ho-te-ri eo-di-jyo?

가까운 호텔이 어디죠?

· Where is the nearest restaurant?

ga-kka-un re-seu-to-rang-i eo-di-jyo?

가까운 레스토랑이 어디죠?

· Where is the nearest café?

ga-kka-un ka-pe-ga eo-di-ye-yo?

가까운 카페가 어디죠?

· Where is the nearest subway station?

ga-kka-un jeon-cheo-ryeo-gi eo-di-jyo?

가까운 전철역이 어디죠?

Emergency situation

internet
in-teo-net
인터넷

ATM
hyeon-geum-ji-geup-gi
현금지급기

rent
dae-yeo
대여

convenience store
pyeo-ni-jeom
편의점

drugstore
yak-guk
약국

smoking zone
heu-byeon gu-yeok
흡연구역

Find and speak phrases quickly!

· Where can I use the internet?

in-teo-net sseul su in-neun de i-sseo-yo?
인터넷 쓸 수 있는 데 있어요?

· Where can I use the Wi-Fi?

wa-i-pa-i teo-ji-neun de i-sseo-yo?
와이파이 터지는 데 있어요?

· Where is the ATM?

hyeon-geum-ji-geup-gi eo-di-sseo-yo?
현금지급기 어딨어요?

· Where is the convenience store?

pyeo-ni-jeom eo-di-sseo-yo?
편의점 어딨어요?

· Where is the drugstore?

yak-guk eo-di-sseo-yo?
약국 어딨어요?

· Do you have aspirin?

a-seu-pi-rin i-sseo-yo?
아스피린 있어요?

· Do you have pills for period?

saeng-ni-tong ya-gi i-sseo-yo?
생리통 약 있어요?

· Where is the smoking zone?

heu-byeon gu-yeok eo-di-ye-yo?
흡연 구역 어디예요?

· Do you have a lighter?

ra-i-teo i-sseu-se-yo?
라이터 있으세요?

How to Use the Airport Railway

You can take the airport railway to get to Seoul quickly. The airport railway has both a direct train that goes straight to Seoul Station and a regular train that stops at other stations.

If you take the direct train, you can go straight from Incheon Airport to Seoul Station. If you want to get to the center of Seoul quickly with comfortable seating, try using the direct train.

If you want a cheaper option, you can also use the regular train (subway). This train passes through 11 subway stations, including Gongdeok Station and Hongik Univ. Station, so you can use the regular train if it stops at a station close to your destination.

You can get more detailed information on the airport railway website at https://www.arex.or.kr

On the street

Frequently used words on the street

01 **Where is**
eo-di-sseo-yo?
어딨어요?

02 **How do I go?**
eo-tteo-ke ga-yo?
어떻게 가요?

03 **way**
gil
길

04 **find**
cha-ja-yo
찾아요

05 **address**
ju-so
주소

06 **map**
ji-do
지도

07 **right**
o-reun-jjok
오른쪽

08 **left**
oen-jjok
왼쪽

09 **block**
gu-yeok
구역

10 **street**
geo-ri
거리

11	corner	mo-tung-i 모퉁이
12	alley	gol-mok 골목
13	crosswalk	hoeng-dan-bo-do 횡단보도
14	walk	geo-reo-yo 걸어요
15	How long	eol-ma-na geol-lyeo-yo? 얼마나 걸려요?
16	Thank you	go-ma-wo-yo 고마워요

Find and speak phrases quickly!

Where is... ?　eo-di-sseo-yo?
어딨어요?

· Where is this?
yeo-gi eo-di-sseo-yo?
여기 어딨어요?

· Where is this restaurant?
i re-seu-to-rang eo-di-sseo-yo?
이 레스토랑 어딨어요?

· Where is this department store?
i bae-kwa-jeom eo-di-sseo-yo?
이 백화점 어딨어요?

· Where is this museum?
i bang-mul-gwan eo-di-sseo-yo?
이 박물관 어딨어요?

· Where is this art gallery?
i mi-sul-gwan eo-di-sseo-yo?
이 미술관 어딨어요?

· Where is the bus stop?
beo-seu jeong-nyu-jang eo-di-sseo-yo?
버스 정류장 어딨어요?

· Where is the subway station?
jeon-cheo-ryeok eo-di-sseo-yo?
전철역 어딨어요?

· Where is the taxi stand?

taek-si jeong-nyu-jang eo-di-sseo-yo?
택시 정류장 어딨어요?

How do I go... eo-tteo-ke ga-yo?
어떻게 가요?

· How do I get here?

yeo-gi eo-tteo-ke ga-yo?
여기 어떻게 가요?

· How do I go to this address?

i ju-so-ro eo-tteo-ke ga-yo?
이 주소로 어떻게 가요?

· How do I go to this building?

i geon-mul eo-tteo-ke ga-yo?
이 건물 어떻게 가요?

· How do I go to this restaurant?

i re-seu-to-rang eo-tteo-ke ga-yo?
이 레스토랑 어떻게 가요?

· How do I go to this museum?

i bang-mul-gwan eo-tteo-ke ga-yo?
이 박물관 어떻게 가요?

How do I go to the bus stop?

beo-seu jeong-nyu-jang eo-tteo-ke ga-yo?
버스 정류장 어떻게 가요?

How do I go to the subway station?

jeon-cheo-ryeok eo-tteo-ke ga-yo?
전철역 어떻게 가요?

How do I go to the taxi stand?

taek-si jeong-nyu-jang eo-tteo-ke ga-yo?
택시 정류장 어떻게 가요?

way

gil
길

Is this the right way?

i gi-ri ma-ja-yo?
이 길이 맞아요?

Can you show me the way?

gil jom al-lyeo-jul su i-sseo-yo?
길 좀 알려줄 수 있어요?

Is this the right direction?

i bang-hyang-i ma-ja-yo?
이 방향이 맞아요?

I think it's the wrong way.

i gi-ri a-nin geot ga-ta-you
이 길이 아닌 것 같아요.

find cha-ja-yo
찾아요

· I gotta find this.
jeo yeo-gi cha-ja-yo
저 여기 찾아요.

· I gotta find this address.
i ju-so cha-ja-yo
이 주소 찾아요.

· I gotta find this restaurant.
i re-seu-to-rang cha-ja-yo
이 레스토랑 찾아요.

· I gotta find a bus stop.
beo-seu jeong-nyu-jang cha-ja-yo
버스 정류장 찾아요.

· I gotta find a taxi stand.
taek-si jeong-nyu-jang cha-ja-yo
택시 정류장 찾아요.

· I gotta find a subway station.
jeon-cheo-ryeok cha-ja-yo
전철역 찾아요.

address ju-so
주소

· Where is this address?
i ju-so eo-di-ye-yo?
이 주소 어디예요?

| · How do I get to this address? | **i ju-so eo-tteo-ke ga-yo?**
이 주소 어떻게 가요? |
| · You know this address? | **i ju-so a-se-yo?**
이 주소 아세요? |

map

ji-do
지도

| · Is this map right? | **i ji-do-ga ma-ja-yo?**
이 지도가 맞아요? |
| · Is this the location on the map? | **ji-do-ui yeo-gi-ga yeo-gi-in-ga-yo?**
지도의 여기가 여기인가요? |

right

o-reun-jjok
오른쪽

| · Go right. | **o-reun-jjo-geu-ro ga-yo**
오른쪽으로 가요. |
| · Go right at the corner. | **o-reun-jjok mo-tung-i-reul do-ra-yo**
오른쪽 모퉁이를 돌아요. |

· Go straight to the right.	**o-reun-jjo-geu-ro gye-sok ga-yo** 오른쪽으로 계속 가요.
· It's the building on the right.	**o-reun-jjok geon-mu-ri-e-yo** 오른쪽 건물이에요.

left   oen-jjok
왼쪽

· Go left.	**oen-jjo-geu-ro ga-yo** 왼쪽으로 가요.
· Go left at the corner.	**oen-jjok mo-tung-i-reul do-ra-yo** 왼쪽 모퉁이를 돌아요.
· Go straight to the left.	**oen-jjo-geu-ro gye-sok ga-yo** 왼쪽으로 계속 가요.
· It's the building on the left.	**oen-jjok geon-mu-ri-e-yo** 왼쪽 건물이에요.

block

gu-yeok
구역

· Go around this block.

i gu-yeo-geul do-ra-seo ga-yo
이 구역을 돌아서 가요.

· Go straight down this block.

i gu-yeo-geul tta-ra jjuk nae-ryeo ga-se-yo
이 구역을 따라 쭉 내려 가세요.

· The building is on the next block.

geu bil-ding-eun da-eum gu-yeo-ge i-sseo-yo
그 빌딩은 다음 구역에 있어요.

street

geo-ri
거리

· Go straight down this street.

i geo-ri-reul tta-ra jjuk nae-ryeo ga-yo
이 거리를 따라 쭉 내려 가요.

· It's on the next street.

i da-eum geo-ri-e i-sseo-yo
이 다음 거리에 있어요.

corner mo-tung-i
모퉁이

· It's around the corner.	**i mo-tung-i-reul dol-myeon i-sseo-yo** 이 모퉁이를 돌면 있어요.
· I've heard that it's around the corner.	**yeo-gi dol-myeon it-da-go haen-neun-de…** 여기 돌면 있다고 했는데….
· Is there this building around the corner?	**yeo-gi dol-myeon i geon-mu-ri i-sseo-yo?** 여기 돌면 이 건물이 있어요?
· Not this corner, around the next corner.	**yeo-gi mal-go da-eum mo-tung-i-ye-yo** 여기 말고 다음 모퉁이예요.

alley gol-mok
골목

· Should I go into this alley?	**i gol-mo-geu-ro deu-reo-ga-yo?** 이 골목으로 들어가요?

· Go into this alley.

i gol-mo-geu-ro deu-reo-ga-yo
이 골목으로 들어가요.

· Not this alley.

i gol-mo-geun a-ni-e-yo
이 골목은 아니에요.

· It's the next alley.

da-eum gol-mo-gi-e-yo
다음 골목이에요.

crosswalk

hoeng-dan-bo-do
횡단보도

· Where is the crosswalk?

hoeng-dan-bo-do-ga eo-di-ye-yo?
횡단보도 어디예요?

· Is the crosswalk far from here?

hoeng-dan-bo-do meo-reo-yo?
횡단보도 멀어요?

· You gotta cross here.

yeo-gi-seo geon-neo-ya dwae-yo
여기서 건너야 돼요.

walk 🚶

geo-reo-yo
걸어요

· Can I walk from here?

yeo-gi-seo geo-reo-gal su i-sseo-yo?
여기서 걸어갈 수 있어요?

· How long should I walk for?

eol-ma-na geo-reo-yo?
얼마나 걸어요?

· I don't like walking, anything else I can take?

geot-gi si-reun-de mwo ta-myeon dwae-yo?
걷기 싫은데 뭐 타면 돼요?

How long 🕑?

eol-ma-na geol-lyeo-yo?
얼마나 걸려요?

· How long does it take from here?

yeo-gi-seo eol-ma-na geol-lyeo-yo?
여기서 얼마나 걸려요?

· How long does it take by walking?

geo-reo-seo eol-ma-na geol-lyeo-yo?
걸어서 얼마나 걸려요?

How long does it take by bus?	**beo-seu-ro eol-ma-na geol-lyeo-yo?** 버스로 얼마나 걸려요?
How long does it take by subway?	**jeon-cheol-lo eol-ma-na geol-lyeo-yo?** 전철로 얼마나 걸려요?
How long does it take by taxi?	**taek-si-ro eol-ma-na geol-lyeo-yo?** 택시로 얼마나 걸려요?

Thank you go-ma-wo-yo
고마워요

| Thank you. | **go-ma-wo-yo**
고마워요. |
| Thanks for your help. | **do-wa-jwo-seo go-ma-wo-yo**
도와줘서 고마워요. |

Emergency situation

lost
gi-reul i-reo-sseo-yo
길을 잃었어요

robbed
so-mae-chi-gi-ya!
소매치기야!

public restroom
gong-jung-hwa-jang-sil
공중화장실

No money
jeo don eop-seo-yo
저 돈 없어요

Find and speak phrases quickly!

· I got lost.

jeo gi-reul i-reo-sseo-yo
저 길을 잃었어요.

· I'm a traveler. Can you help me?

jeo yeo-haeng-gae-gin-de do-wa-ju-se-yo
저 여행객인데 도와주세요.

· I've been robbed!

so-mae-chi-gi dang-hae-sseo-yo!
소매치기 당했어요!

· Call the police!

gyeong-chal bul-leo-jwo-yo!
경찰 불러줘요!

· There's a thief! Get him!

jeo-gi do-du-gi-e-yo! ja-ba!
저기 도둑이에요! 잡아!

· Where is the public restroom?

gong-jung-hwa-jang-sil eo-di in-na-yo?
공중화장실 어디 있나요?

· May I please use the restroom?

hwa-jang-sil jom sseo-do doe-na-yo?
화장실 좀 써도 되나요?

· I'm really in a hurry.

jeo jeong-mal.... geu-pae-yo
저 정말…. 급해요.

· I got no money.   **jeo don eop-seo-yo**
저 돈 없어요.

· Really.   **jin-jja-ye-yo**
진짜예요.

· I'm gonna yell!   **so-ri ji-reul geo-ye-yo!**
소리 지를 거예요!

memo

How to Use the Naver Map App

① After installing the application, tap the menu bar in the upper left corner.

② Tap the Settings icon in the upper right corner.

③ Tap "Language".

④ Select the language you prefer: Korean, English, Chinese, or Japanese.

⑤ In the search bar, type in your destination and select the appropriate option from the list.

⑥ Make sure the location is correct and tap "To".

⑦ Results for the best routes will appear. As your means of transportation, you can choose public transportation, car, bike, or walking.

⑧ If you want to use either the bus or subway only, tap "Bus" or "Subway" accordingly.

⑨ You can also select a specific departure time. (Select a route to view the detailed directions.)

⑩ Double tap the "My Location" button and zoom in on the map. Now, you can easily see which direction you are facing. (Try turning while holding your phone!)

In a taxi &
On the bus

Frequently used words in a taxi and on the bus

01 **taxi stand**
taek-si jeong-nyu-jang
택시 정류장

02 **take me to ~**
(location)eu-ro/ro ga ju-se-yo
(location)으로/로 가 주세요

03 **address**
ju-so
주소

04 **staring fare**
gi-bon yo-geum
기본 요금

05 **fare**
yo-geum
요금

06 **trunk**
teu-reong-keu
트렁크

07 **faster**
ppal-li ga ju-se-yo
빨리 가 주세요

08 **pull over**
se-wo-ju-se-yo
세워주세요

09 **change**
jan-don
잔돈

10 **credit card**
sin-yong-ka-deu
신용카드

11	bus stop	beo-seu jeong-nyu-jang 버스 정류장
12	bus for ~	(destination)haeng beo-seu (destination)행 버스
13	other side	ban-dae-jjok 반대쪽
14	wait	gi-da-ryeo-yo 기다려요
15	bus fare	beo-seu yo-geum 버스 요금
16	transfer	hwan-seung 환승
17	get off	nae-ryeo-yo 내려요
18	stop	jeong-geo-jang 정거장

Find and speak phrases quickly!

taxi stand   taek-si jeong-nyu-jang
택시 정류장

· Where is the taxi stand?

taek-si jeong-nyu-jang eo-di-ye-yo?
택시 정류장 어디예요?

· Is the taxi stand close?

taek-si jeong-nyu-jang-i ga-kka-wo-yo?
택시 정류장이 가까워요?

· Where do I get a taxi?

taek-si eo-di-seo tal su i-sseo-yo?
택시 어디서 탈 수 있어요?

· Can I walk to the taxi stand?

taek-si jeong-nyu-jang geo-reo-gal su- i-sseo-yo?
택시 정류장 걸어갈 수 있어요?

take me to ~

(location)eu-ro/ro ga ju-se-yo

(location)으로/로 가 주세요

· Take me here.

yeo-gi-ro ga ju-se-yo
여기로 가 주세요.

· Take me to this address.

i ju-so-ro ga ju-se-yo
이 주소로 가 주세요.

· Take me to this hotel.

i ho-tel-lo ga ju-se-yo
이 호텔로 가 주세요.

· Take me to this museum.

i bang-mul-gwan-eu-ro ga ju-se-yo
이 박물관으로 가 주세요.

· Take me to this art gallery.

i mi-sul-gwan-eu-ro ga ju-se-yo
이 미술관으로 가 주세요.

· Take me to this park.

i gong-won-eu-ro ga ju-se-yo
이 공원으로 가 주세요.

· Take me downtown.

si-nae-ro ga ju-se-yo
시내로 가 주세요.

· Take me to the airport.

gong-hang-eu-ro ga ju-se-yo
공항으로 가 주세요.

111

address

ju-so
주소

· Take me to this address.
i ju-so-ro ga ju-se-yo
이 주소로 가 주세요.

· Do you know where this address is?
i ju-so eo-din-ji a-se-yo?
이 주소 어딘지 아세요?

· This address is weird.
i ju-so-ga i-sang-hae-yo
이 주소가 이상해요.

· Take me to the nearest spot to this address.
i ju-so-e-seo ga-kka-un de-ro ga ju-se-yo
이 주소에서 가까운 데로 가 주세요.

staring fare

gi-bon yo-geum
기본 요금

· How much is the starting fare?
gi-bon yo-geu-mi eol-ma-ye-yo?
기본 요금이 얼마예요?

· The starting fare is too expensive.
gi-bon yo-geum bi-ssa-yo
기본 요금 비싸요.

fare **yo-geum**
요금

· How much is the fare?

yo-geu-mi eol-ma-ye-yo?
요금이 얼마예요?

· How much do I owe you?

yo-geum eol-ma deu-ryeo-ya doe-jyo?
요금 얼마 드려야 되죠?

· The fare is too expensive.

yo-geu-mi bi-ssa-yo
요금이 비싸요.

· I'll pay by cash.

hyeon-geu-meu-ro hal-ge-yo
현금으로 할게요.

trunk **teu-reong-keu**
트렁크

· Please open the trunk.

teu-reong-keu yeo-reo ju-se-yo
트렁크 열어 주세요.

· The trunk is not opening.

teu-reong-keu an yeol-lyeo-yo
트렁크 안 열려요.

113

| · Please help me put this in. | i-geo neon-neun geot jom do-wa-ju-se-yo |
| | 이거 넣는 것 좀 도와주세요. |

faster

ppal-li ga ju-se-yo

빨리 가 주세요

· Can you go faster?	ppal-li ga ju-sil su in-na-yo?
	빨리 가 주실 수 있나요?
· Please go faster.	ppal-li ga ju-se-yo
	빨리 가 주세요.
· I gotta go faster.	ppal-li ga-ya dwae-yo
	빨리 가야 돼요.

pull over

se-wo ju-se-yo

세워주세요

· Pull over here.	yeo-gi-seo se-wo-ju-se-yo
	여기서 세워주세요.
· Pull over at the crosswalk.	hoeng-dan-bo-do-e-seo se-wo-ju-se-yo
	횡단보도에서 세워주세요.

114

· Pull over just around the corner.

mo-tung-i do-ra-seo se-wo-ju-se-yo
모퉁이 돌아서 세워주세요.

change jan-don
잔돈

· Keep the change.

jan-do-neun dwae-sseo-yo
잔돈은 됐어요.

· Why aren't you giving me the change?

jan-don wae an jwo-yo?
잔돈 왜 안 줘요?

· Please give me in coins.

dong-jeon-eu-ro ju-se-yo
동전으로 주세요.

credit card sin-yong-ka-deu
신용카드

· Do you take credit cards?

sin-yong-ka-deu doe-na-yo?
신용카드 되나요?

· I have cash.

hyeon-geum i-sseo-yo
현금 있어요.

· I don't have cash.   **hyeon-geum eop-seo-yo**
현금 없어요.

bus stop   beo-seu jeong-nyu-
                       jang
                       버스정류장

· Where is the bus   **beo-seu-jeong-nyu-jang**
stop?   **eo-di-ye-yo?**
                      버스정류장 어디예요?

· Is the bus stop   **beo-seu jeong-nyu-jang**
close?   **ga-kka-wo-yo?**
                      버스 정류장 가까워요?

· Where do I get a   **beo-seu eo-di-seo tal su**
bus?   **i-sseo-yo?**
                      버스 어디서 탈 수 있어요?

· Can I walk to the bus **beo-seu jeong-nyu-jang**
stop?   **geo-reo-gal su i-sseo-yo?**
                      버스 정류장 걸어갈 수 있어요?

bus for (destination)haeng beo-seu

(destination)행 버스

· Is this a bus for downtown?

i-geo si-nae ga-neun beo-seu-ye-yo?

이거 시내 가는 버스예요?

· Is this a bus for the airport?

i-geo gong-hang ga-neun beo-seu-ye-yo?

이거 공항 가는 버스예요?

· Is this the bus for the subway station?

i-geo jeon-cheol-yeok ga-neun beo-seu-ye-yo?

이거 전철역 가는 버스예요?

other side ban-dae-jjok

반대쪽

· You gotta go ride on the other side.

ban-dae-jjo-ge-seo ta-ya doem-ni-da

반대쪽에서 타야 됩니다.

· How do I get to the other side?

ban-dae-jjo-geu-ro ga-ryeo-myeon eo-di-ro ga-yo?

반대쪽으로 가려면 어디로 가요?

· Does the bus on the other side go downtown?

ban-dae-jjok beo-seu-ga si-nae-e ga-yo?
반대쪽 버스가 시내에 가요?

wait | gi-da-ryeo-yo
기다려요

· How long do I wait?

eol-ma-na gi-da-ryeo-yo?
얼마나 기다려요?

· You gotta wait for 10 minutes.

sip-bun gi-da-ri-se-yo
10(십)분 기다리세요.

· Don't wait. It doesn't come here.

gi-da-ri-ji ma-se-yo yeo-gi an wa-yo
기다리지 마세요. 여기 안 와요.

bus fare | beo-seu yo-geum
버스 요금

· How much is the bus fare?

beo-seu yo-geu-mi eol-ma-ye-yo?
버스 요금이 얼마예요?

· Can I pay in cash?

beo-seu yo-geum hyeon-geum-eu-ro nae-yo?
버스 요금 현금으로 내요?

· How do I pay for the fare?

beo-seu yo-geu-meun eo-tteo-ke nae-yo?
버스 요금은 어떻게 내요?

transfer   **hwan-seung**
환승

· Where do I transfer?

eo-di-seo hwan-seung-hae-yo?
어디서 환승해요?

· Which bus should I transfer to?

myeot beo-neu-ro hwan-seung-hae-yo?
몇 번으로 환승해요?

get off   **nae-ryeo-yo**
내려요

· I get off here.

jeo yeo-gi-seo nae-ryeo-yo
저 여기서 내려요.

· Where do I get off?

jeo eo-di-seo nae-ryeo-yo?
저 어디서 내려요?

· Do I get off here?

yeo-gi-seo nae-ri-neun geo ma-ja-yo?

여기서 내리는 거 맞아요?

· Let me know when to get off.

nae-ryeo-ya hal ttae al-lyeo-ju-se-yo

내려야 할 때 알려주세요.

stop 🚏

jeong-geo-jang

정거장

· How many stops do I go?

myeot jeong-geo-jang ga-ya dwae-yo?

몇 정거장 가야 돼요?

· Do I get off at this stop?

i-beon jeong-geo-jang-e-seo nae-ri-na-yo?

이번 정거장에서 내리나요?

Emergency situation

window
chang-mun
창문

door
mun
문

detour
do-ra-ga-da
돌아가다

miss
mot nae-ryeo-sseo-yo
못 내렸어요!

stop button
bel
벨

Find and speak phrases quickly!

· Do you mind opening the window?
chang-mun jom yeo-reo-do doe-jyo?
창문 좀 열어도 되죠?

· The window is stuck.
chang-mu-ni an yeol-lyeo-yo
창문이 안 열려요.

· I can't open the door.
mu-ni an yeol-lyeo-yo
문이 안 열려요.

· Why are you detouring?
wae do-ra-ga-yo?
왜 돌아가요?

· I think you're detouring!
do-ra-ga-neun geo ga-teun-de-yo!
돌아가는 거 같은데요!

· It's too expensive.
bi-ssa-yo
비싸요.

· I missed my stop.
jeo mot nae-ryeo-sseo-yo
저 못 내렸어요.

· I should get off here!
yeo-gi-seo nae-ryeo-ya doe-neun-de!
여기서 내려야 되는데!

· Pull over, please!
se-wo-jwo-yo!
세워줘요!

· Where is the bell?	**ha-cha-bel eo-di i-sseo-yo?** 벨 어디 있어요?
· Could you press the stop button?	**bel jom nul-lyeo-ju-sil-lae-yo?** 벨 좀 눌러주실래요?
· You should have pressed the stop button!	**be-reul nul-leo-sseo-ya-jyo!** 벨을 눌렀어야죠!
· I did press the stop button!	**bel nul-leot-geo-deun-yo!** 벨 눌렀거든요!
· Open the door.	**mun jom yeo-reo-ju-se-yo** 문 좀 열어주세요.
· The door won't open.	**mu-ni an yeol-lyeo-yo** 문이 안 열려요.
· The door is not closed.	**mu-ni an da-tyeo-sseo-yo** 문이 안 닫혔어요.
· My scarf is stuck in the door.	**mu-ne seu-ka-peu-ga kki-eo-sseo-yo!** 문에 스카프가 끼었어요!
· Could you close the window?	**chang-mun jom da-da-ju-sil-lae-yo?** 창문 좀 닫아주실래요?

Do you mind opening the window?	**chang-mun yeo-reo-do doe-na-yo?**
창문 열어도 되나요?	
I can't close the window.	**chang-mun-eul da-deul su-ga eop-seo-yo**
창문을 닫을 수가 없어요.	
I can't open the window.	**chang-mun-eul yeol su-ga eop-seo-yo**
창문을 열 수가 없어요.	
Excuse me, your hair is stuck in the window.	**jeo-gi-yo, chang-mu-ne meo-ri-ka-ra-gi kki-eo-sseo-yo**
저기요, 창문에 머리카락이 끼었어요.	

A Must-Have Item for Your Trip to Korea, T-money

One of the most convenient transportation tools for traveling in Korea is a "T-Money" card. A T-Money card can be used on buses, subways, and taxis in Korea.
Purchasing a T-money Card at a Convenience Store
You can buy T-Money cards at convenience stores.
The price of the cards ranges from ₩3,000 to ₩6,000, depending on their design.

Charging T-Money Cards
After purchasing a card, you must charge it to use it. You can charge your T-Money card at subway stations or convenience stores. You can ask a store worker to charge the amount you want right after you buy a card at the convenience store. Or, you can charge it at the transportation card charging machines located inside subway stations.

On the subway &
On the train

On the subway & train

01 **subway station**
jeon-cheol-lyeok
전철역

02 **train station**
gi-cha-yeok
기차역

03 **ticket window**
mae-pyo-so
매표소

04 **ticket machine**
bal-gwon-gi
발권기

05 **fare**
yo-geum
요금

06 **express train**
geu-paeng nyeol-cha
급행열차(KTX)

07 **one-way**
pyeon-do
편도

08 **round trip**
wang-bok
왕복

09 **ticket to ~**
(destination) ga-neun pyo
(destination) 가는 표

10	timetable	si-gan-pyo 시간표
11	platform	seung-gang-jang 승강장
12	transfer	hwan-seung 환승
13	get off	nae-ryeo-yo 내려요
14	line	ho-seon (number)호선
15	subway map	no-seon-do 노선도
16	seat	ja-ri 자리

Find and speak phrases quickly!

subway station

전철역

· Where is the subway station?

jeon-cheo-ryeok eo-di-ye-yo?
전철역 어디예요?

· How do I get to the subway station?

jeon-cheo-ryeok eo-tteo-ke ga-yo?
전철역 어떻게 가요?

· Is this the subway station?

yeo-gi-ga jeon-cheo-ryeo-gi-e-yo?
여기가 전철역이에요?

· Is the subway station far from here?

jeon-cheo-ryeo-gi yeo-gi-seo meo-reo-yo?
전철역 여기서 멀어요?

train station

gi-cha-yeok
기차역

· Where is the train station?

gi-cha-yeok eo-di-ye-yo?
기차역 어디예요?

· How do I get to the train station?

gi-cha-yeok-eo-tteo-ke ga-yo?
기차역 어떻게 가요?

· Is this the train
station?

yeo-gi-ga gi-cha-yeo-gi-e-yo?
여기가 기차역이에요?

· Is the train station far
from here?

gi-cha-yeo-gi yeo-gi-seo meo-reo-yo?
기차역이 여기서 멀어요?

ticket window mae-pyo-so
매표소

· Where is the ticket
window?

mae-pyo-so eo-di-ye-yo?
매표소 어디예요?

· How do I get to the
ticket window?

mae-pyo-so eo-tteo-ke ga-yo?
매표소 어떻게 가요?

· I'm gonna buy a
ticket.

pyo sal geo-ye-yo
표 살 거예요.

ticket machine

bal-kwon-gi
발권기

· Where is the ticket
machine?

bal-gwon-gi eo-di-sseo-yo?
발권기 어딨어요?

131

How do I use the
ticket machine?

**bal-gwon-gi eo-tteo-ke
sseo-yo?**
발권기 어떻게 써요?

The ticket machine is
not working.

**bal-gwon-gi an doe-neun-
de-yo**
발권기 안 되는데요.

Help me use this
machine.

**bal-gwon-gi sseu-neun
geot jom do-wa-jwo-yo**
발권기 쓰는 것 좀 도와줘요.

My ticket is not
coming out.

je pyo-ga an na-wa-yo
제 표가 안 나와요.

fare

yo-geum
요금

How much is the
fare?

yo-geum eol-ma-ye-yo?
요금 얼마예요?

Do you take credit
cards?

**sin-yong-ka-deu doe-na-
yo?**
신용카드 되나요?

I don't have any
cash.

hyeon-geum eop-seo-yo
현금 없어요.

express train geu-paeng-nyeol-cha
급행 열차(KTX)

· Is there an express train to here?

yeo-gi-ro ga-neun geu-paeng-nyeol-cha(KTX) i-sseo-yo?
여기로 가는 급행열차(KTX) 있어요?

· How much is the express train(KTX)?

geu-paeng-nyeol-cha(KTX) eol-ma-ye-yo?
급행열차(KTX)는 얼마예요?

· Where should I go for the express train(KTX)?

geu-paeng-nyeol-cha(KTX) eo-di-seo ta-yo?
급행열차(KTX) 어디서 타요?

· What time is the express train(KTX)?

geu-paeng-nyeol-cha(KTX) myeot si-e i-sseo-yo?
급행열차(KTX) 몇 시에 있어요?

one-way pyeon-do
편도

· Two tickets, one-way please.

pyeon-do-ro 2(du)jang ju-se-yo
편도로 2(두)장 주세요.

· I said a one-way ticket.	**pyeon-do-ro dal-la-go hae-sseo-yo** 편도로 달라고 했어요.
· This is not a one-way ticket.	**i-geo pyeon-do pyo a-nin-de-yo** 이거 편도 표 아닌데요.
· Is this a one-way ticket?	**i-geo pyeon-do pyo ma-ja-yo?** 이거 편도 표 맞아요?
· Can I change this into a one-way ticket?	**i-geo pyeon-do-ro ba-kkul su i-sseo-yo?** 이거 편도로 바꿀 수 있어요?

round-trip

wang-bok
왕복

· One ticket, round-trip please.	**wang-bo-geu-ro 1(han)-jang-i-yo** 왕복으로 1(한)장이요.
· I said a round trip ticket.	**wang-bo-geu-ro dal-la-go hae-sseo-yo** 왕복으로 달라고 했어요.

· This is not a round trip ticket

i-geo wang-bok pyo a-nin-de-yo

이거 왕복 표 아닌데요.

· Is this a round-trip ticket?

i-geo wang-bok pyo ma-ja-yo?

이거 왕복 표 맞아요?

· Can I change this into a round-trip ticket?

i-geo wang-bo-geu-ro ba-kkul su i-sseo-yo?

이거 왕복으로 바꿀 수 있어요?

ticket to ~ (destination)

ga-neun pyo (destination)

가는 표

· One ticket, to here.

yeo-gi ga-neun pyo han jang i-yo

여기 가는 표 한 장이요.

· How much is the ticket to here?

yeo-gi ga-neun pyo eol-ma-ye-yo?

여기 가는 표 얼마예요?

timetable si-gan-pyo
시간표

· Where can I see the timetable?
si-gan-pyo eo-di-seo bwa-yo?
시간표 어디서 봐요?

· Show me the timetable.
si-gan-pyo bo-yeo ju-se-yo
시간표 보여 주세요.

· The timetable is too confusing.
si-gan-pyo-ga bok-ja-pae-yo
시간표가 복잡해요.

· Please help me look at this timetable.
si-gan-pyo bo-neun geot jom do-wa-jwo-yo
시간표 보는 것 좀 도와줘요.

platform seung-gang-jang
승강장

· Where is platform two?
2(i)-beon seung-gang-jang eo-di-ye-yo?
2(이)번 승강장 어디예요?

· I can't find the platform.
seung-gang-jang-eul mot chat-ge-sseo-yo
승강장을 못 찾겠어요.

136

transfer 🚏 hwan-seung
환승

· Where do I transfer?

hwan-seung-ha-neun de-eo-di-ye-yo
환승하는 데 어디예요?

· Do I transfer here?

hwan-seung yeo-gi-seo hae-yo?
환승 여기서 해요?

· Do I transfer to get here?

yeo-gi-ro ga-ryeo-myeon hwan-seung-hae-ya dwae-yo?
여기로 가려면 환승해야 돼요?

· Do I get off here to transfer?

hwan-seung-ha-ryeo-myeon yeo-gi-seo nae-ryeo-yo?
환승하려면 여기서 내려요?

---

get off 🚶 nae-ryeo-yo
내려요

· Get off here.

yeo-gi-seo nae-ri-se-yo
여기서 내리세요.

137

· Don't get off here.

yeo-gi-seo nae-ri-myeon an doem-ni-da

여기서 내리면 안 됩니다.

· Do I get off here?

yeo-gi-seo nae-ri-myeon doe-na-yo?

여기서 내리면 되나요?

· You gotta get off here.

i yeo-ge-seo nae-ryeo-ya doem-ni-da

이 역에서 내려야 됩니다.

line

(number)ho-seon

(number)호선

· I'm going here, which line should I take?

yeo-gi gal geon-de myeot ho-seon ta-yo?

여기 갈 건데 몇 호선 타요?

· Will this line get me here?

i no-seon ta-myeon yeo-gi ga-na-yo?

이 노선 타면 여기 가나요?

· I'm transferring to this line.

i no-seo-neu-ro ga-ra-tal geo-ye-yo

이 노선으로 갈아탈 거예요.

subway map no-seon-do
노선도

· Where is the subway map?

no-seon-do-neun eo-di in-na-yo?
노선도는 어디 있나요?

· Can I get a subway map?

no-seon-do ha-na ba-deul su in-na-yo?
노선도 하나 받을 수 있나요?

· Please help me look at this subway map.

no-seon-do bo-neun geot jom do-wa-ju-se-yo
노선도 보는 것 좀 도와주세요.

seat ja-ri
자리

· Is this seat taken?

ja-ri i-sseo-yo?
자리 있어요?

· Can I sit here?

yeo-gi-an-ja-do doe-na-yo?
여기 앉아도 되나요?

· Could you move your bag?

ga-bang jom chi-wo ju-sil-lae-yo?
가방 좀 치워 주실래요?

Emergency situation

lost
bun-sil
분실

ticket
pyo
표

wrong way
da-reun bang-hyang
다른 방향

Find and speak phrases quickly!

· I lost my ticket.
pyo-reul bun-sil-hae-sseo-yo
표를 분실했어요.

· I lost my bag.
ga-bang-eul bun-sil-hae-sseo-yo
가방을 분실했어요.

· left my bag on the subway.
ji-ha-cheo-re ga-bang-eul no-ko nae-ryeo-sseo-yo
지하철에 가방을 놓고 내렸어요.

· Where is the lost & found?
bun-sil-mul sen-teo-ga eo-di-ye-yo?
분실물 센터가 어디예요?

· My ticket is gone.
je pyo-ga eop-seo-jyeo-sseo-yo
제 표가 없어졌어요.

· I got the wrong ticket.
pyo-reul jal-mot sa-sseo-yo
표를 잘못 샀어요.

· I got the wrong subway.
ji-ha-cheol jal-mot ta-sseo-yo
지하철 잘못 탔어요.

· I got on the wrong line.
ho-seo-neul jal-mot ta-sseo-yo
호선을 잘못 탔어요.

memo

Rail Pass for Foreign Tourists, Korail Pass

The "Korail Pass" is recommended for travelers who want to visit multiple cities during their stay in Korea. The Korail Pass is an exclusive ticket for foreign tourists, and it allows for unlimited use of all trains operated by Korail for a certain period of time. It is a great option that allows travelers to freely visit various parts of Korea.

The Korail Pass offers different durations for usage, ranging from 1 to 10 days. It is available for purchase in advance online. All trains operated by Korail are included, such as KTX (the high-speed train) and Mugunghwa trains. You can create a pass by making a reservation at the link below.

https://www.letskorail.com

In a hotel

Frequently used words in a hotel

01 **lobby**
ro-bi
로비

02 **reservation**
ye-yak
예약

03 **check-in**
che-keu-in
체크인

04 **bed**
chim-dae
침대

05 **view**
jeon-mang
전망

06 **breakfast**
jo-sik
조식

07 **how much ~**
eol-ma
얼마

08 **elevator**
el-li-be-i-teo
엘리베이터

09 **which floor**
myeot cheung
몇 층

10 **room key**
bang ki
방 키

11	baggage	jim
		짐
12	my room	nae bang
		내 방
13	towel	su-geon
		수건
14	toothbrush	chit-sol
		칫솔
15	pillow	be-gae
		베개
16	dryer	deu-ra-i-gi
		드라이기
17	bathtub	yok-jo
		욕조
18	water	mul
		물
19	internet	in-teo-net
		인터넷

20	television	tel-le-bi-jeon
		텔레비전
21	clean	cheong-so
		청소
22	wake-up call	mo-ning kol
		모닝 콜
23	room service	rum seo-bi-seu
		룸 서비스
24	safe	gae-in geum-go
		개인 금고
25	laundry	se-tak
		세탁
26	ice	eo-reum
		얼음
27	check-out	che-keu-aut
		체크아웃
28	bill	gye-san-seo
		계산서

29	extra	chu-ga 추가
30	minibar	mi-ni ba 미니 바
31	charge	yo-geum 요금
32	credit card	sin-yong-ka-deu 신용카드
33	taxi	taek-si 택시
34	airport	gong-hang 공항

Find and speak phrases quickly!

lobby 　　　robi
로비

· Where is the lobby?　**ro-bi-ga eo-di-ye-yo?**
로비가 어디예요?

· I can't find the lobby.　**ro-bi-reul mot chat-gen-neun-de-yo**
로비를 못 찾겠는데요.

reservation 　ye-yak
예약

· I got a reservation.　**ye-ya-kae-sseo-yo**
예약했어요.

· I got no reservation.　**ye-yak an hae-sseo-yo**
예약 안 했어요.

· I got a reservation through this website.　**i sai-teu-ro ye-ya-kaen-neun-de-yo**
이 사이트로 예약했는데요.

· I got a reservation under my name, (your name).　**ye-yak (your name) eu-ro/ro hae-sseo-yo**
예약 (your name)으로/로 했어요.

150

check-in

che-keu-in
체크인

- Check-in, please.

che-keu-in ha-ryeo-go-yo
체크인 하려고요.

- Where should I check-in?

che-keu-in eo-di-seo hae-yo?
체크인 어디서 해요?

- What time is the check-in?

che-keu-in myeot si-e ha-na-yo?
체크인 몇 시에 하나요?

- Keep my baggage before I check-in, please.

che-keu-in ha-gi jeon-e jim ma-ta-ju-se-yo
체크인 하기 전에 짐 맡아주세요.

bed

chim-dae
침대

- A single bed, please.

sing-geul chim-dae-ro ju-se-yo
싱글 침대로 주세요.

- A double bed, please.

deo-beul chim-dae-ro ju-se-yo
더블 침대로 주세요.

Twin beds, please.	**teu-win chim-dae-ro ju-se-yo**
	트윈 침대로 주세요.
Get me twin beds, but as one.	**teu-win chim-dae-reul ha-na-ro bu-tyeo jwo-yo**
	트윈 침대를 하나로 붙여 줘요.
Get me the biggest bed.	**je-il keun chim-dae ju-se-yo**
	제일 큰 침대 주세요.
How much is the room with the biggest bed?	**jeil keun chim-dae in-neun bang-eun eol-ma-ye-yo?**
	제일 큰 침대 있는 방은 얼마예요?

view

jeon-mang

전망

I want an ocean view.	**ba-da jeon-mang-eu-ro jwo-yo**
	바다 전망으로 줘요.
I want a city view.	**do-sim jeon-mang-eu-ro jwo-yo**
	도심 전망으로 줘요.

· I want a room with a nice view.	**jeon-mang jo-eun de-ro jwo-yo** 전망 좋은 데로 줘요.
· The view isn't good enough.	**jeon-mang-i byeol-lo-ye-yo** 전망이 별로예요.

breakfast 🍴

jo-sik
조식

· Where do I have breakfast?	**jo-si-geun eo-di-seo meo-geo-yo?** 조식은 어디서 먹어요?
· What time is breakfast?	**jo-si-geun myeot si-ye-yo?** 조식은 몇 시예요?
· What do you have for the breakfast?	**jo-si-geu-ro mwo-ga it-jyo?** 조식으로 뭐가 있죠?
· What time does breakfast end?	**jo-si-geun myeot si-kka-ji-ye-yo?** 조식 몇 시까지예요?

· How much is it
including breakfast?

**jo-sik po-ham-ha-myeon
eol-ma-ye-yo?**

조식 포함하면 얼마예요?

how much **?**   eol-ma

얼마

· How much is it for
one night?

1(il)ba-ge eol-ma-ye-yo?

1(일)박에 얼마예요?

· How much is it for
two nights?

2(i)ba-ge eol-ma-ye-yo?

2(이)박에 얼마예요?

· Can I get a discount?

**ha-rin ba-deul su i-sseo-
yo?**

할인 받을 수 있어요?

· How much is it
including breakfast?

**jo-sik po-ham-ha-myeon
eol-ma-ye-yo?**

조식 포함하면 얼마예요?

· How much is it for an
upgrade?

**eop-geu-re-i-deu-ha-
myeon eol-ma-ye-yo?**

업그레이드하면 얼마예요?

elevator

el-li-be-i-teo
엘리베이터

· Where is the elevator?

el-li-be-i-teo eo-di i-sseo-yo?
엘리베이터 어디 있어요?

· The elevator won't open.

el-li-be-i-teo-ga an yeol-lyeo-yo
엘리베이터가 안 열려요.

· Which one is the lobby button?

1(il)cheung beo-teun-i eo-tteon geo-jyo?
1(일)층 버튼이 어떤 거죠?

· I wanna go to the lobby.

ro-bi ga-ryeo-go-yo
로비 가려고요.

which floor

myeot cheung
몇 층

· Which floor is my room?

je bang myeot cheung-i-e-yo?
제 방 몇 층이에요?

· Which floor has a vending machine?

ja-pan-gi myeot cheung-e i-sseo-yo?
자판기 몇 층에 있어요?

· Which floor has the swimming pool?	**su-yeong-jang myeot cheung-e i-sseo-yo?** 수영장 몇 층에 있어요?
· Which floor has the spa?	**seu-pa myeot cheung-e i-sseo-yo?** 스파 몇 층에 있어요?
· It's the first floor.	**1(il)cheung-i-e-yo** 1(일)층이에요.
· It's the second floor.	**2(i)cheung-i-e-yo** 2(이)층이에요.
· It's the third floor.	**3(sam)cheung-i-e-yo** 3(삼)층이에요.
· It's the fourth floor.	**4(sa)-cheung-i-e-yo** 4(사)층이에요.

room key 🔑	**bang ki** 방 키
· Can I get one more room key?	**bang ki ha-na deo ju-se-yo** 방 키 하나 더 주세요.
· My room key is gone.	**bang ki eop-seo-jyeo-sseo-yo** 방 키 없어졌어요.

156

· My room key is not working.	**bang ki-ga an dwae-yo** 방 키가 안 돼요.

baggage   jim
짐

· Can you keep my baggage?	**jim mat-gil su i-sseo-yo?** 짐 맡길 수 있어요?
· Can you move up my baggage?	**jim ol-lyeo ju-sil su i-sseo-yo?** 짐 올려 주실 수 있어요?
· This is not my baggage.	**i-geo je jim-i a-ni-e-yo** 이거 제 짐이 아니에요.
· My baggage is gone.	**je jim-i eop-seo-jyeo-sseo-yo** 제 짐이 없어졌어요.
· Please find my baggage.	**je jim jom cha-ja ju-se-yo** 제 짐 좀 찾아 주세요.
· Keep my baggage before I check-in, please.	**che-keu-in-ha-gi jeon-e jim jom mat-gyeo ju-se-yo** 체크인하기 전에 짐 좀 맡겨 주세요.

my room

nae bang
내 방

· Where is my room?
nae bang-i eo-di-ye-yo?
내 방이 어디죠?

· I can't find my room.
nae bang-eul mot chat-ge-sseo-yo
내 방을 못 찾겠어요.

· My room is too dark.
nae bang-i eo-du-wo-yo
내 방이 어두워요.

· My room is too bright.
nae bang-i neo-mu bal-ga-yo
내 방이 너무 밝아요.

· My room is too hot.
nae bang-i neo-mu deo-wo-yo
내 방이 너무 더워요.

· My room is too cold.
nae bang-i neo-mu chu-wo-yo
내 방이 너무 추워요.

· My room is smelly.
nae bang-e-seo naem-sae na-yo
내 방에서 냄새나요.

towel   su-geon
수건

· More towels, please.   **su-geon deo ju-se-yo**
수건 더 주세요.

· I got no towels.   **su-geon eop-seo-yo**
수건 없어요.

· My towels are dirty.   **su-geon deo-reo-wo-yo**
수건 더러워요.

· I want clean towels.   **su-geon kkae-kkeu-tan geol-lo ju-se-yo**
수건 깨끗한 걸로 주세요.

· I want bigger towels.   **keun su-geon-eu-ro ju-se-yo**
큰 수건으로 주세요.

toothbrush   chit-sol
칫솔

· I got no toothbrush.   **chit-sol eop-seo-yo**
칫솔 없어요.

· Get me a toothbrush.   **chit-sol ju-se-yo**
칫솔 주세요.

· Get me one more toothbrush.	**chit-sol ha-na deo ju-se-yo** 칫솔 하나 더 주세요.
· Get me some toothpaste.	**chi-yak ju-se-yo** 치약 주세요.
· Get me a toothbrush for kids.	**eo-rin-i-yong chit-sol ju-se-yo** 어린이용 칫솔 주세요.
· You got toothpaste for kids?	**eo-rin-i-yong chi-yak i-sseo-yo?** 어린이용 치약 있어요?
· You got a softer toothbrush?	**bu-deu-reo-un chit-sol eom-na-yo?** 부드러운 칫솔 없나요?
· You got a dental floss?	**chi-sil i-sseo-yo?** 치실 있어요?

pillow

begae
베개

· Get me one more pillow.	**be-gae ha-na deo ju-se-yo** 베개 하나 더 주세요.

· My pillow is too hard.	**be-gae-ga neo-mu ttak-tta-kae-yo** 베개가 너무 딱딱해요.
· My pillow is too thick.	**be-gae-ga neo-mu no-pa-yo** 베개가 너무 높아요.
· My pillow is too · thin.	**be-gae-ga neo-mu na-ja-yo** 베개가 너무 낮아요.
· You got a bigger pillow?	**be-gae keun geo i-sseo-yo?** 베개 큰 거 있어요?

dryer

deu-ra-i-gi
드라이기

· Get me a dryer.	**deu-ra-i-gi ju-se-yo** 드라이기 주세요.
· I got no dryer.	**deu-ra-i-gi eop-seo-yo** 드라이기 없어요.
· The dryer is broken.	**deu-ra-i-gi go-jang-na-sseo-yo** 드라이기 고장났어요.

· The dryer is not working.

deu-ra-i-gi jal an dwae-yo
드라이기 잘 안 돼요.

bathtub

yok-jo
욕조

· My bathtub is dirty.

yok-jo-ga deo-reo-wo-yo
욕조가 더러워요.

· Clean my bathtub, please.

yok-jo da-kka-ju-se-yo
욕조 닦아주세요.

· The water in the bathtub won't go down.

yok-jo mu-ri jal an ppa-jyeo-yo
욕조 물이 잘 안 빠져요.

water

mul
물

· There's something wrong with the water tap.

mu-ri an na-wa-yo
물이 안 나와요.

· The water is too hot.

mu-ri neo-mu tteu-geo-wo-yo
물이 너무 뜨거워요.

· The water is too cold.	**mu-ri neo-mu cha-ga-wo-yo** 물이 너무 차가워요.
· I can't adjust the water temperature.	**mul on-do jo-jeo-ri an dwae-yo** 물 온도 조절이 안 돼요.
· There's no water coming out from the shower.	**sya-wo-gi-e-seo mu-ri an na-wa-yo** 샤워기에서 물이 안 나와요.
· The toilet won't flush.	**byeon-gi mu-ri an nae-ryeo-ga-yo** 변기 물이 안 내려가요.

internet

in-teo-net
인터넷

· The internet is not working.	**in-teo-net an dwae-yo** 인터넷 안 돼요.
· Where can I use the internet?	**in-teo-net hal su in-neun de eo-di-ye-yo?** 인터넷 할 수 있는 데 어디예요?

· I can't get the Wi-Fi. **wa-i-pa-i-ga an teo-jyeo-yo**
와이파이가 안 터져요.

· Where can I use a computer? **keom-pyu-teo sseul su in-neun de eo-di-ye-yo?**
컴퓨터 쓸 수 있는 데 어디예요?

television tel-le-bi-jeon
텔레비전

· The television is not working. **tel-le-bi-jeon-i an na-wa-yo**
텔레비전이 안 나와요.

· I can't get the cable channels. **ke-i-beu-ri an na-wa-yo**
케이블이 안 나와요.

· The TV remote control is not working. **ri-mo-keo-ni an dwae-yo**
리모컨이 안 돼요.

· How do I control the volume? **eum-nyang jo-jeol eo-tteo-ke hae-yo?**
음량 조절 어떻게 해요?

· I can't adjust the channel. **chae-neol jo-jeo-ri jal an dwae-yo**
채널 조절이 안 돼요.

164

clean

cheong-so
청소

· Clean my room.

cheong-so-hae ju-se-yo
청소해 주세요.

· Nobody cleaned my room.

bang cheong-so an doe-eo i-sseo-yo
방 청소 안 되어 있어요.

· You don't have to clean my room.

cheong-so-neun an hae ju-syeo-do doem-ni-da
청소는 안 해 주셔도 됩니다.

· Clean my room in the afternoon.

o-hu-e cheong-so-hae ju-se-yo
오후에 청소해 주세요.

· Nobody cleaned the restroom.

hwa-jang-sil cheong-so-ga an doe-eo i-sseo-yo
화장실 청소가 안 되어 있어요.

· The rubbish bin is not empty.

sseu-re-gi-tong-i an bi-wo-jyeo i-sseo-yo
쓰레기통이 안 비워져 있어요.

wake-up call mo-ning kol
모닝 콜

· I want a wake-up call.

mo-ning kol hae ju-se-yo
모닝 콜 해 주세요.

· Make it at seven.

7(il-gop)si-e hae ju-se-yo
7(일곱)시에 해 주세요.

· I wanna cancel my wake-up call.

mo-ning kol chwi-so-hal-ge-yo
모닝 콜 취소할게요.

· I want two wake-up calls in a row.

mo-ning kol yeon-da-ra du beon hae ju-se-yo
모닝 콜 연달아 두 번 해 주세요.

room service 👁 rum seo-bi-seu
룸 서비스

· I wanna order room service.

rum seo-bi-seu si-kil-ge-yo
룸 서비스 시킬게요.

· I wanna see the room service menu.

rum seo-bi-seu me-nyu bo-go si-peo-yo
룸 서비스 메뉴 보고 싶어요.

· I want my breakfast brought up to my room.	**rum seo-bi-seu-ro a-chim gat-da ju-se-yo**
	룸 서비스로 아침 갖다 주세요.
· I want some wine brought up to my room.	**rum seo-bi-seu-ro wa-in gat-da ju-se-yo**
	룸 서비스로 와인 갖다 주세요.

safe

gae-in geum-go
개인 금고

· How do I use the safe?	**gae-in geum-go eo-tteo-ke sseo-yo?**
	개인 금고 어떻게 써요?
· The safe won't open.	**gae-in geum-go an yeol-lyeo-yo**
	개인 금고 안 열려요.
· There's something in the safe.	**gae-in geum-go-e mwo-ga i-sseo-yo**
	개인 금고에 뭐가 있어요.

laundry 🔲

se-tak
세탁

· I want a laundry service.

se-tak seo-bi-seu sin-cheong-hal-ge-yo
세탁 서비스 신청할게요.

· When is the laundry service coming?

se-tak seo-bi-seu eon-je wa-yo?
세탁 서비스 언제 와요?

· My laundry is damaged.

se-tang-mu-ri mang-ga-jyeo-sseo-yo
세탁물이 망가졌어요.

ice 🎲

eo-reum
얼음

· There's no ice.

eo-reum-i eop-seo-yo
얼음이 없어요.

· Where do I get the ice?

eo-reum eo-di-seo ga-jyeo-wa-yo?
얼음 어디서 가져와요?

· Get me some ice.

eo-reum jom gat-da ju-se-yo
얼음 좀 갖다 주세요.

check-out

che-keu-aut
체크아웃

· Check-out, please.	**che-keu-aut hal-ge-yo** 체크아웃 할게요.
· What time is the check-out?	**che-keu-aut myeot si-ye-yo?** 체크아웃 몇 시예요?
· I wanna extend one more day.	**ha-ru deo yeon-jang-hal-ge-yo** 하루 더 연장할게요.
· I wanna check-out later.	**che-keu-aut jom i-tta hal-ge-yo** 체크아웃 좀 이따 할게요.

bill

gye-san-seo
계산서

· Show me the bill.	**gye-san-seo bo-yeo ju-se-yo** 계산서 보여 주세요.
· The bill is wrong.	**gye-san-seo teul-lyeo-sseo-yo** 계산서 틀렸어요.

· I want a detailed bill.

ja-se-han gye-san-seo
jom bo-yeo ju-se-yo
자세한 계산서 좀 보여 주세요.

extra ➕

chu-ga
추가

· Here's the extra
charge.

chu-ga yo-geum-i bu-
teon-neun-de-yo
추가 요금이 붙었는데요.

· What's the extra
charge here?

eo-tteon ge chu-ga-doen
geo-ye-yo?
어떤 게 추가된 거예요?

· Explain this extra
charge.

i chu-ga yo-geum seol-
myeong-hae ju-se-yo
이 추가 요금 설명해 주세요.

minibar

mi-ni ba
미니 바

· I didn't use the
minibar.

mi-ni ba i-yong an haen-
neun-de-yo
미니 바 이용 안 했는데요.

· I only had water from the minibar.	**mi-ni ba-e-seo mul-man ma-syeo-sseo-yo** 미니 바에서 물만 마셨어요.
· I only had a beer from the minibar.	**mini ba-e-seo maek-ju-man ma-syeo-sseo-yo** 미니 바에서 맥주만 마셨어요.
· The minibar charge is not right.	**mini ba yo-geum-i jal-mot-dwae-sseo-yo** 미니 바 요금이 잘못됐어요.

charge

yo-geum
요금

· What's this charge for?	**i yo-geum-eun mwo-jyo?** 이 요금은 뭐죠?
· I think this amount isn't right.	**yo-geum-i deo na-on geot ga-teun-de-yo** 요금이 더 나온 것 같은데요.
· The total charge doesn't add up.	**yo-geum hap-gye-ga teul-lyeo-sseo-yo** 요금 합계가 틀렸어요.

credit card 🪪 card sin-yong-ka-deu

신용카드

· Do you take credit cards?

sin-yong-ka-deu doe-na-yo?

신용카드 되나요?

· Your credit card doesn't work.

sin-yong-ka-deu an geul-kyeo-yo

신용카드 안 긁혀요.

· I don't have any other credit card.

da-reun sin-yong-ka-deu eop-seo-yo

다른 신용카드 없어요.

· Please try one more time.

han beon deo geul-geo-bwa ju-se-yo

한 번 더 긁어봐 주세요.

· I don't have any cash.

hyeon-geum eop-seo-yo

현금 없어요.

· Can I get a discount?

ha-rin eom-na-yo?

할인 없나요?

taxi

taek-si
택시

· Please call a taxi.

taek-si jom bul-leo ju-se-yo
택시 좀 불러 주세요.

· Is taking a taxi expensive?

taek-si bi-ssan ga-yo?
택시 비싼가요?

· Where are you gonna go?

taek-si-ro eo-di ga-si-ge-yo?
택시로 어디 가시게요?

airport

gong-hang
공항

· I'm going to the airport.

gong-hang gal geo-ye-yo
공항 갈 거예요.

· What should I take to the airport?

gong-hang ga-ryeo-myeon mwo ta-yo?
공항 가려면 뭐 타요?

· Is there a bus going to the airport?

gong-hang ga-neun beo-seu i-sseo-yo?
공항 가는 버스 있어요?

173

Emergency situation

not working
go-jang-i-e-yo
고장이에요

not coming
an na-wa-yo
안 나와요

can't open
an yeol-lyeo-yo
안 열려요

robbed
do-duk ma-ja-sseo-yo
도둑맞았어요

stuck
ga-tyeo-sseo-yo
갇혔어요

sick
a-pa-yo
아파요

lost
i-reo-beo-ryeo-sseo-yo
잃어버렸어요

ambulance
eung-geup-cha
응급차

Find and speak phrases quickly!

· The dryer is not working.
deu-ra-i-eo-ga go-jang-i-e-yo
드라이어가 고장이에요.

· The television is not working.
tel-le-bi-jeon-i go-jang-i-e-yo
텔레비전이 고장이에요.

· The computer is not working.
keom-pyu-teo-ga go-jang-i-e-yo
컴퓨터가 고장이에요.

· The phone is not working.
jeon-hwa-gi-ga go-jang-i-e-yo
전화기가 고장이에요.

· The shower hose is not working.
sya-wo-gi-ga go-jang-i-e-yo
샤워기가 고장이에요.

· The bidet is not working.
bi-de-ga go-jang-i-e-yo
비데가 고장이에요.

· I can't open the door.
mun-i an yeol-lyeo-yo
문이 안 열려요.

· I can't open the safe.
geum-go-ga an yeol-lyeo-yo
금고가 안 열려요.

· I can't open the curtains.
keo-teu-ni an yeol-lyeo-yo
커튼이 안 열려요.

I'm stuck in the room.	**bang-e ga-tyeo-sseo-yo** 방에 갇혔어요.
I'm stuck in the elevator.	**el-li-be-i-teo-e ga-tyeo-sseo-yo** 엘리베이터에 갇혔어요.
I'm stuck in the bathroom.	**hwa-jang-si-re ga-tyeo-sseo-yo** 화장실에 갇혔어요.
I lost my room key.	**bang ki-reul i-reo-beo-ryeo-sseo-yo** 방 키를 잃어버렸어요.
I lost my coupon.	**ku-po-neul i-reo-beo-ryeo-sseo-yo** 쿠폰을 잃어버렸어요.
I lost my passport.	**yeo-gwo-neul i-reo-beo-ryeo-sseo-yo** 여권을 잃어버렸어요.
I lost my phone.	**jeon-hwa-gi-reul i-reo-beo-ryeo-sseo-yo** 전화기를 잃어버렸어요.
I lost my laptop.	**no-teu-bu-geul i-reo-beo-ryeo-sseo-yo** 노트북을 잃어버렸어요.

· I lost my shoes.	**sin-ba-reul i-reo-beo-ryeo-sseo-yo** 신발을 잃어버렸어요.
· I lost my valuables.	**gwi-jung-pu-meul i-reo-beo-ryeo-sseo-yo** 귀중품을 잃어버렸어요.
· The elevator is not coming here.	**el-li-be-i-teo-ga an wa-yo** 엘리베이터가 안 와요.
· My meal is not here yet.	**sik-sa-ga an na-wa-yo** 식사가 안 나와요.
· My room service is not here yet.	**rum seo-bi-seu-ga an wa-yo** 룸 서비스가 안 와요.
· My laundry is not here yet.	**se-tak seo-bi-seu-ga an wa-yo** 세탁 서비스가 안 와요.
· Water is not coming out.	**mu-ri an na-wa-yo** 물이 안 나와요.
· I can't get the cable on.	**kei-beu-ri an na-wa-yo** 케이블이 안 나와요.
· My bag was robbed.	**je ga-bang do-duk-ma-ja-sseo-yo** 제 가방 도둑맞았어요.

· My baggage was robbed.	**je jim do-duk-ma-ja-sseo-yo** 제 짐 도둑맞았어요.
· I feel sick.	**so-gi an jo-a-yo** 속이 안 좋아요.
· I have a stomachache.	**bae-ga a-pa-yo** 배가 아파요.
· I have a headache.	**meo-ri-ga a-pa-yo** 머리가 아파요.
· I broke my arm.	**pa-ri bu-reo-jyeo-sseo-yo** 팔이 부러졌어요.
· I broke my leg.	**da-ri-ga bu-reo-jyeo-sseo-yo** 다리가 부러졌어요.
· Call an ambulance.	**eung-geup-cha bul-leo-ju-se-yo** 응급차 불러주세요.

Rest for My Soul, Temple Stay

If you're looking for a unique experience while traveling in Korea, we highly recommend a Temple Stay. Temple Stay literally means "staying for a certain period" at a Korean Buddhist temple. While doing so, you can enjoy traditional experience programs that allow you to learn about the history and culture of Korean Buddhism. There are various types of Temple Stay programs. If you are unable to stay overnight, there are "special programs" that allow you to experience Korean Buddhist culture within just a few hours. There are also "hands-on programs" that offer a variety of traditional Korean and Buddhist cultural activities, such as traditional tea making and cultural heritage tours. And for those looking to relax their weary body and mind, there are also "rest programs."

If you want to know more about Temple Stays or make a reservation, please visit the link below.

https://www.templestay.com

At a restaurant or café

Frequently used words at a restaurant or café

01 **two**
du myeong-i-yo
두 명이요

02 **reservation**
ye-yak
예약

03 **table**
te-i-beul
테이블

04 **order**
ju-mun
주문

05 **menu**
me-nyu
메뉴

06 **recommendation**
chu-cheon
추천

07 **spoon / chopsticks**
sut-ga-rak / jeot-ga-rak
숟가락 / 젓가락

08 **drink**
eum-nyo
음료

09 **napkin**
hyu-ji
휴지

10	check	gye-san 계산
11	to go (in the restaurant)	po-jang 포장
12	restroom	hwa-jang-sil 화장실
13	Wi-Fi	wa-i-pa-i 와이파이
14	meat	go-gi 고기
15	Korean food	han-guk eum-sik 한국 음식
16	It's spicy	mae-wo-yo 매워요
17	food I can't eat	mot meong-neun eum-sik 못 먹는 음식
18	side dish	ban-chan 반찬

Find and speak phrases quickly!

two 🧍🧍
2(du)myeong-i-yo
2(두)명이요

· A table for two.
2(du)myeong-i-yo
2(두)명이요.

· Only me.
hon-ja-ye-yo
혼자예요.

reservation 📞
ye-yak
예약

· I got a reservation.
ye-ya-kae-sseo-yo
예약했어요.

· I got no reservation.
ye-yak an hae-sseo-yo
예약 안 했어요.

· I got a reservation for two.
2(du)myeong-eu-ro ye-ya-kae-sseo-yo
2(두)명으로 예약했어요.

· I got a reservation under name (your name).
(i-reum)eu-ro/ro ye-ya-kae-sseo-yo
(your name)으로/로 예약했어요.

table te-i-beul
테이블

· The table is too dirty.
te-i-beu-ri deo-reo-wo-yo
테이블이 더러워요.

· Could you please wipe the table?
te-i-beul da-kka-ju-se-yo
테이블 닦아주세요.

· The table is wobbling.
te-i-beul heun-deul-geo-ryeo-yo
테이블 흔들거려요.

· The table is too small.
te-i-beul neo-mu jo-ba-yo
테이블 너무 좁아요.

· Get me another table.
da-reun ja-ri-ro ju-se-yo
다른 자리로 주세요.

· Please give me a seat by the window.
chang-ga ja-ri-ro ju-se-yo
창가 자리로 주세요.

order ju-mun
주문

· Excuse me!
yeo-gi-yo!
여기요!

· Excuse me!
jeo-gi-yo!
저기요!

186

· Excuse me, sir/ ma'am!	**sa-jang-nim!** 사장님!
· I'd like to order now.	**ju-mun-hal-ge-yo** 주문할게요
· I already ordered.	**ju-mun-hae-sseo-yo** 주문했어요.
· I already ordered mine ages ago.	**ju-mun-han ji han-cham dwae-sseo-yo** 주문한 지 한참 됐어요.
· Are you ready to order?	**ju-mun-ha-si-ge-sseo-yo?** 주문하시겠어요?

menu

me-nyu
메뉴

| · What would you like from the menu? | **me-nyu eo-tteon geol-lo ha-sil-lae-yo?** 메뉴 어떤 걸로 하실래요? |
| · Do you have anything special? | **teuk-byeol-han me-nyu-ga in-na-yo?** 특별한 메뉴가 있나요? |

187

· I got the wrong menu.

me-nyu jal-mot na-wa-sseo-yo

메뉴 잘못 나왔어요.

recommendation chu-cheon

추천

· Could you give us some recommendations?

me-nyu chu-cheon-hae ju-sil su in-na-yo?

메뉴 추천해 주실 수 있나요?

· What's the most popular menu?

mwo-ga je-il jal na-ga-yo?

뭐가 제일 잘 나가요?

· Which one of these two do you recommend?

i dul jung-e mwol chu-cheon-ha-se-yo?

이 둘 중에 뭘 추천하세요?

spoon / chopsticks sut-ga-rak / jeot-ga-rak

숟가락 / 젓가락

· There's no spoon/chopsticks.

sut-ga-ra-gi/jeot-ga-ra-gi eop-seo-yo

숟가락이/젓가락이 없어요.

· I dropped the spoon/
chopsticks.

**sut-ga-ra-geul/jeot-ga-ra-
geul tteo-reo-tteu-ryeo-
sseo-yo**

숟가락을/젓가락을 떨어뜨렸어요.

· There's something
on the spoon/
chopsticks.

**sut-ga-ra-ge/jeot-ga-
ra-ge mwo-ga mu-deo
i-sseo-yo**

숟가락에/젓가락에 뭐가 묻어 있어요.

· Can I get another
spoon/chopsticks,
please?

**sut-ga-rak/jeot-ga-rak ha-
na deo ju-se-yo**

숟가락/젓가락 하나 더 주세요.

· I'm not very good at
using chopsticks.

**je-ga jeot-ga-rak-ji-reul
mo-tae-yo**

제가 젓가락질을 못해요.

· You got a fork?

hok-si po-keu in-na-yo?

혹시 포크 있나요?

drink

eum-nyo

음료

· What kind of drinks
you got?

**eum-nyo-neun eo-tteon
ge i-sseo-yo?**

음료는 어떤 게 있어요?

· I'll have a Coke.	**kol-la ju-se-yo** 콜라 주세요.
· I'll have a Sprite.	**sa-i-da ju-se-yo** 사이다 주세요.
· I'll have a beer.	**maek-ju ju-se-yo** 맥주 주세요.
· I'll have a soju.	**so-ju ju-se-yo** 소주 주세요.
· I'll have a makgeolli.	**mak-geol-li ju-se-yo** 막걸리 주세요.

napkin

hyu-ji
휴지

· There's no napkin.	**hyu-ji-ga eop-seo-yo** 휴지가 없어요.
· Please get me some napkins.	**hyu-ji jom ju-se-yo** 휴지 좀 주세요.
· Please get me more napkins.	**hyu-ji deo ju-se-yo** 휴지 더 주세요.
· You got some wet tissue?	**mul-ti-syu i-sseo-yo?** 물티슈 있어요?

check 📋

gye-san
계산

· Check, please.

gye-san-hal-ge-yo
계산할게요.

· The bill is incorrect.

yeong-su-jeung-i jal-mot-dwae-sseo-yo
영수증이 잘못됐어요.

· I never ordered this menu.

i me-nyu an si-kyeo-sseo-yo
이 메뉴 안 시켰어요.

· Would you like the receipt?

yeong-su-jeung deu-ril-kka-yo?
영수증 드릴까요?

· Please give me the receipt.

yeong-su-jeung ju-se-yo
영수증 주세요.

· Do you take cards?

ka-deu doe-na-yo?
카드 되나요?

· I'll pay in cash.

hyeon-geu-meu-ro hal-ge-yo
현금으로 할게요.

to go

po-jang

포장

· Is it for here or to go?

deu-si-go ga-se-yo? a-ni-myeon po-jang-ha-sil geo-ye-yo?

드시고 가세요? 아니면 포장하실 거예요?

· To go.

po-jang-i-e-yo

포장이에요.

· I'll eat here.

yeo-gi-seo meo-geul geo-ye-yo

여기서 먹을 거예요.

· Could you pack the leftover food for me, please?

na-meun eum-sik po-jang-hae ju-sil su in-na-yo?

남은 음식 포장해 주실 수 있나요?

· Please pack this for me.

i-geo po-jang-hae ju-se-yo

이거 포장해 주세요.

restroom hwa-jang-sil
화장실

· Where is the
restroom?

hwa-jang-sil eo-di i-sseo-yo?

화장실 어디 있어요?

· Is someone in the
restroom?

hwa-jang-si-re nu-gu i-sseo-yo?

화장실에 누구 있어요?

· The restroom is
locked.

hwa-jang-sil mu-ni an yeol-lyeo-yo

화장실 문이 안 열려요.

· What's the restroom
password?

hwa-jang-sil bi-mil-beon-ho-ga mwo-ye-yo?

화장실 비밀번호가 뭐예요?

· There's no toilet
paper in the
restroom.

hwa-jang-si-re hyu-ji-ga eop-seo-yo

화장실에 휴지가 없어요.

· There's no soap in
the restroom.

hwa-jang-si-re bi-nu-ga eop-seo-yo

화장실에 비누가 없어요.

Wi-Fi 📶

wa-i-pa-i
와이파이

· Do you have Wi-Fi here?

yeo-gi wa-i-pa-i doe-na-yo?
여기 와이파이 되나요?

· What's the Wi-Fi password?

wa-i-pa-i bi-mil-beon-ho mwo-ye-yo?
와이파이 비밀번호 뭐예요?

· Can I get the Wi-Fi password?

wa-i-pa-i bi-mil-beon-ho jom al-lyeo-ju-se-yo
와이파이 비밀번호 좀 알려주세요.

· I can't connect to the Wi-Fi.

wa-i-pa-i yeon-gyeo-ri an dwae-yo
와이파이 연결이 안 돼요.

meat

go-gi
고기

· Could we get two servings of pork belly?

sam-gyeop-sal 2(i)-in-bun ju-se-yo
삼겹살 2인분 주세요.

· I'd like to add one portion of pork neck.	**mok-sal 1(il)-in-bun chu-ga-hal-ge-yo** 목살 1인분 추가할게요.
· Is it okay to eat this now?	**ji-geum meo-geo-do dwae-yo?** 지금 먹어도 돼요?
· Is this fully cooked?	**i-geo da i-geo-sseo-yo?** 이거 다 익었어요?
· How should I grill this?	**i-geo eo-tteo-ke gu-wo-yo** 이거 어떻게 구워요?
· Could you give me a help?	**jom do-wa-ju-sil su in-na-yo?** 좀 도와주실 수 있나요?
· Get me one more pair of scissors.	**ga-wi ha-na deo ju-se-yo** 가위 하나 더 주세요.
· Get me one more tongs.	**jip-ge ha-na deo ju-se-yo** 집게 하나 더 주세요.
· The heat is too strong.	**bu-ri neo-mu se-yo** 불이 너무 세요.
· The heat is too weak.	**bu-ri neo-mu ya-kae-yo** 불이 너무 약해요.
· Take out the fire.	**bul jom ppae ju-se-yo** 불 좀 빼 주세요.

· Wrap it in lettuce and enjoy.

ssa-me ssa-seo deu-se-yo
쌈에 싸서 드세요.

· How do I wrap it in lettuce?

ssam eo-tteo-ke ssa-yo?
쌈 어떻게 싸요?

· What should I eat with the meat to make it tasty?

go-gi-neun mwo-rang ga-chi meo-geo-ya ma-si-sseo-yo?
고기는 뭐랑 같이 먹어야 맛있어요?

· Dip the meat in ssamjang and enjoy.

go-gi-geun ssam-jamg-e jji-geo deu-se-yo
고기는 쌈장에 찍어 드세요.

Korean food

han-guk eum-sik
한국 음식

· I'd like Dakgalbi in small/medium/large size, please.

dak-gal-bi so/jung/dae ju-se-yo
닭갈비 소/중/대 주세요.

· Could you bring individual plates?

gae-in jeop-si jom ju-se-yo
개인 접시 좀 주세요.

Could you give me a spatula/ladle?	**ju-geok/guk-ja jom ju-se-yo** 주걱/국자 좀 주세요.
Could you explain how to eat this?	**meong-neun bang-beop jom al-lyeo-ju-se-yo** 먹는 방법 좀 알려주세요
Is it okay to eat it now?	**ji-geum meo-geo-do dwae-yo?** 지금 먹어도 돼요?
Eat your vegetables first.	**ya-chae-bu-teo deu-se-yo** 야채부터 드세요.
Please make fried rice.	**bo-kkeum-bap hae ju-se-yo** 볶음밥 해 주세요.
Make fried rice for two, please.	**bo-kkeum-bap 2(i)-in-bun hae ju-se-yo** 볶음밥 2인분 해 주세요.
How spicy would you like it?	**maep-gi jeong-do-neun eo-tteo-ke hae deu-ril-kka-yo?** 맵기 정도는 어떻게 해 드릴까요?

· Mild, please.

an mae-un ma-seu-ro ju-se-yo

안 매운 맛으로 주세요.

· Medium spicy, please.

jung-gan ma-seu-ro ju-se-yo

중간 맛으로 주세요.

· Spicy, please.

mae-un-ma-seu-ro ju-se-yo

매운 맛으로 주세요.

It's spicy.

mae-wo-yo

매워요

· Is this spicy?

i-geo mae-wo-yo?

이거 매워요?

· Does this dish have a spicy flavor?

yeo-gi-e mae-un ma-si in-na-yo?

여기에 매운 맛이 있나요?

· I can't handle spicy food.

jeo-neun mae-un geo mot meo-geo-yo

저는 매운 거 못 먹어요

· Do you have non-spicy dishes?

an mae-un eum-si-gi i-sseo-yo?

안 매운 음식이 있어요?

198

· It's too spicy.	**neo-mu mae-wo-yo** 너무 매워요.
· Please make it less spicy.	**maep-ji an-ke hae ju-se-yo** 맵지 않게 해 주세요.
· I enjoy spicy food.	**jeo-neun mae-un eum-si-geul jo-a-hae-yo** 저는 매운 음식을 좋아해요.
· I can handle spicy food well.	**jeo-neun mae-un eum-si-geul jal meo-geo-yo** 저는 매운 음식을 잘 먹어요.

Food I can't eat

mot meong-neun eum-sik
못 먹는 음식

| · I can't eat (food). | **jeo-neun (food) mot meo-geo-yo**
저는 (food) 못 먹어요. |
| · I have an allergy to (food). | **jeo-neun (food) al-le-reu-gi-ga i-sseo-yo**
저는 (food) 알레르기가 있어요. |

· Does this contain (food)?

yeo-gi-e (food) in-na-yo?
여기에 (food) 있나요?

· Without (food), please.

(food) ppae ju-se-yo
(food) 빼 주세요.

· I am a vegan.

jeo-neun bi-geo-ni-ye-yo
저는 비건이에요.

· I am a vegetarian.

jeo-neun chae-sik-ju-ui-ja-ye-yo
저는 채식주의자예요.

· Do you have any vegan options here?

yeo-gi bi-geon me-nyu-ga in-na-yo
여기 비건 메뉴가 있나요?

side dish

ban-chan
반찬

· Could I have more side dishes, please?

ban-chan jom deo ju-se-yo
반찬 좀 더 주세요.

· Can I get more of this?

i-geo deo ju-se-yo
이거 더 주세요.

· Is it possible to get more of this?

i-geo deo ju-sil su in-na-yo?
이거 더 주실 수 있나요?

self-serve sel-peu
셀프

· You need to get your own water here.	**mu-reun sel-peu** 물은 셀프
· Please use the self-service bar for side dishes.	**ban-cha-neun sel-peu ba-reul i-yong-hae ju-se-yo** 반찬은 셀프 바를 이용해 주세요.
· Where is the self-service bar?	**sel-peu ba eo-di i-sseo-yo?** 셀프 바 어디 있어요?

café menu ka-pe me-nyu
카페 메뉴

· I'll take an iced americano, please.	**a-i-seu a-me-ri-ka-no ha-na ju-se-yo** 아이스 아메리카노 하나 주세요.
· I'll take a café latte, please.	**ra-tte han jan ju-se-yo** 라떼 한 잔 주세요.
· What's the best-selling drink here?	**je-il jal na-ga-neun eum-nyo-ga mwo-ye-yo?** 제일 잘 나가는 음료가 뭐예요?

· Do you have any special menu items?

yeo-gi si-geu-ni-cheo me-nyu in-na-yo?
여기 시그니처 메뉴 있나요?

· Any dessert suggestions?

di-jeo-teu chu-cheon-hae ju-sil su in-na-yo?
디저트 추천해 주실 수 있나요?

· Is there any caffeine in this?

yeo-gi ka-pe-i-ni i-sseo-yo?
여기 카페인이 있어요?

· Can I swap the regular milk for soy milk?

u-yu-reul du-yu-ro byeon-gyeong ga-neug-han-ga-yo?
우유를 두유로 변경 가능한가요?

· Is it possible to switch to lactose-free milk?

hok-si rak-to-peu-ri u-yu-ro byeon-gyeong ga-neung-han-ga-yo?
혹시 락토프리 우유로 변경 가능한가요?

---

to-go

te-i-keu aut
테이크 아웃

· For here or to go?

deu-si-go ga-se-yo?
드시고 가세요?

· I'll take it to go.

te-i-keu-a-ut hal-ge-yo
테이크아웃 할게요.

· You can't use disposable cups inside the store.

il-hoei-yong keo-beun mae-jang a-ne-seo sa-yong-hal su eop-sseum-ni-da
일회용 컵은 매장 안에서 사용할 수 없습니다.

· I'd like to take the remaining drink to go.

na-meun eum-nyo te-i-keu-a-ut hal-ge-yo
남은 음료 테이크아웃 할게요.

Emergency situation

too salty
neo-mu jja-yo
너무 짜요

too hot
neo-mu tteu-geo-wo-yo
너무 뜨거워요

too cold
neo-mu cha-ga-wo-yo
너무 차가워요

too spicy
neo-mu mae-wo-yo
너무 매워요

weird
ma-si i-sang-han-de-yo
맛이 이상한데요

drop
tteo-reo-tteu-ryeo-sseo-yo
떨어뜨렸어요

hasn't come out yet
an na-wan-neun-de-yo
안 나왔는데요

change
ba-kkwo-ju-se-yo
바꿔주세요

wrap up to go
po-jang-hae ju-se-yo
포장해 주세요

didn't order
i-geo an si-kyeo-sseo-yo
이거 안 시켰어요

without

i-geo ppae ju-se-yo

이거 빼 주세요

refill

ri-pil

리필

spilled

heul-lyeo-sseo-yo

흘렸어요

Find and speak phrases quickly!

· This is too salty.

i-geo neo-mu jja-yo
이거 너무 짜요.

· This is too hot.

i-geo neo-mu tteu-geo-wo-yo
이거 너무 뜨거워요

· Careful! The plate is hot.

jo-sim-ha-se-yo! jeop-si tteu-geo-wo-yo
조심하세요! 접시 뜨거워요.

· I almost got burned!

jeo ji-geum de-il ppeon hae-sseo-yo!
저 지금 데일 뻔했어요!

· This is too cold.

i-geo neo-mu cha-ga-wo-yo.
이거 너무 차가워요.

· Heat this up, please.

de-wo ju-se-yo
데워 주세요

· This is too spicy.

i-geo neo-mu mae-wo-yo
이거 너무 매워요.

· This is too bland.

neo-mu sing-geo-wo-yo
너무 싱거워요.

· Get me some salt.

so-geum jom ju-se-yo
소금 좀 주세요.

· This tastes weird.

i-geo ma-si i-sang-han-de-yo

이거 맛이 이상한데요.

· Call the chef, please.

ju-bang-jang bul-leo-jwo-yo

주방장 불러줘요.

· My menu hasn't come out yet.

me-nyu an na-wan-neun-de-yo

메뉴 안 나왔는데요.

· My drink hasn't come out yet.

eum-nyo-ga an na-wa-sseo-yo

음료가 안 나왔어요.

· Please wrap this up to go.

i-geo po-jang-hae-ju-se-yo

이거 포장해주세요.

· I spilled this.

i-geo heul-lyeo-sseo-yo

이거 흘렸어요.

· Clean here, please.

yeo-gi jom da-kka-ju-se-yo

여기 좀 닦아주세요.

· Can you refill this?

ri-pil doe-na-yo?

리필 되나요?

memo

Popular Korean Foods

Bulgogi

Chicken

Kimchi stew

Tteokbokki

Bibimbap

Soybean paste stew

Soy sauce Marinated crab

When sightseeing

Frequently used words when sightseeing

01 **ticket office**
mae-pyo-so
매표소

02 **discount**
ha-rin
할인

03 **entrance**
ip-gu
입구

04 **exit**
chul-gu
출구

05 **admission**
ip-jang-nyo
입장료

06 **recommendation**
chu-cheon
추천

07 **information booth**
an-nae-so
안내소

08 **tourist attraction**
gwan-gwang myeong-so
관광 명소

09 **brochure**
pam-peul-let
팜플렛

10	business hours	yeong-eop si-gan 영업 시간
11	timetable	si-gan-pyo 시간표
12	picture	sa-jin 사진
13	explain	seol-myeong 설명
14	schedule	il-jeong 일정
15	departure	chul-bal 출발
16	arrival	do-chak 도착
17	translation	tong-yeok 통역
18	city tour	si-ti tu-eo 시티 투어

19	map	ji-do 지도
20	gift shop	seon-mul ga-ge 선물 가게
21	performance	gong-yeon 공연
22	reservation	ye-mae 예매
23	show time	gong-yeon si-gan 공연 시간
24	sold out	mae-jin 매진
25	seat	jwa-seok 좌석
26	intermission	hyu-sik si-gan 휴식 시간
27	subtitle	ja-mak 자막

28	main actor	ju-yeon bae-u 주연배우
29	backstage	mu-dae dwi 무대 뒤
30	No	geum-ji 금지
31	restroom	hwa-jang-sil 화장실

Find and speak phrases quickly!

ticket office

mae-pyo-so
매표소

· Where is the ticket office?

mae-pyo-so eo-di-ye-yo?
매표소 어디예요?

· Is the ticket office close?

mae-pyo-so ga-kka-wo-yo?
매표소 가까워요?

discount

ha-rin
할인

· Can I get a discount?

ha-rin-doe-na-yo?
할인되나요?

· Can I get a student discount?

hak-saeng ha-rin-doe-na-yo?
학생 할인되나요?

· Is this the discounted price?

ha-rin-doen ga-gyeok-i-e-yo?
할인된 가격이에요?

entrance ip-gu
입구

- Where is the entrance? **ip-gu-ga eo-di-ye-yo?**
입구가 어디예요?

- I can't see the entrance. **ip-gu-ga an bo-yeo-yo**
입구가 안 보여요.

- Is this the direction to the entrance? **i bang-hyang-i ip-gu-ye-yo?**
이 방향이 입구예요?

exit chul-gu
출구

- Where is the exit? **chul-gu-ga eo-di-jyo?**
출구가 어디죠?

- I can't see the exit. **chul-gu-ga an bo-yeo-yo**
출구가 안 보여요.

- Is this the direction to the exit? **i bang-hyang-i chul-gu-ye-yo?**
이 방향이 출구예요?

admission ip-jang-nyo
입장료

How much is the admission?

ip-jang-nyo-ga eol-ma-jyo?
입장료가 얼마죠?

How much is the admission fee for children?

eo-ri-ni ip-jang-nyo-neun eol-ma-jyo?
어린이 입장료는 얼마죠?

Does the admission cover everything?

ip-jang-nyo-man nae-myeon da bol su in-na-yo?
입장료만 내면 다 볼 수 있나요?

recommendation chu-cheon
추천

Do you have a recommendation on what to see?

chu-cheon-hal man-han bol-geo-ri i-sseo-yo?
추천할 만한 볼거리 있어요?

What do you most recommend to see?

je-il chu-cheon-ha-neun geon mwo-ye-yo?
제일 추천하는 건 뭐예요?

· Could you recommend a route?

chu-cheon-ha-neun ko-seu-ga in-na-yo?

추천하는 코스가 있나요?

information booth

an-nae-so

안내소

· Where is the information booth?

an-nae-so-ga eo-di-ye-yo?

안내소가 어디예요?

· Is the information booth far from here?

an-nae-so-ga yeo-gi-seo meo-reo-yo?

안내소가 여기서 멀어요?

· Where is the closest information booth?

ga-kka-un an-nae-so-neun eo-di-ye-yo?

가까운 안내소는 어디예요?

tourist attraction gwan-gwang myeong-so
관광 명소

· What's the most famous tourist attraction here?

je-il yu-myeong-han gwan-gwang myeong-so-ga eo-tteon-geo-jyo?
제일 유명한 관광 명소가 어떤거죠?

· Please recommend a tourist attraction.

gwan-gwang myeong-so chu-cheon-hae ju-se-yo
관광 명소 추천해 주세요.

· Which one takes less time to see?

bo-neun si-ga-ni jeok-ge geol-li-neun geon eo-tteon-geo-ye-yo?
보는 시간이 적게 걸리는 건 어떤 거죠?

brochure pam-peul-let
팜플렛

· Where can I get the brochure?

pam-peul-le-seun eo-di-seo gu-hae-yo?
팜플렛은 어디서 구해요?

· Get me a brochure.

pam-peul-let ha-na ju-se-yo
팜플렛 하나 주세요.

· You got a brochure? **pam-peul-let i-sseo-yo?**
팜플렛 있어요?

business hours yeong-eop si-gan
영업 시간

· What are the
business hours? **yeong-eop si-ga-ni eon-je-ye-yo?**
영업 시간이 언제예요?

· What time do you
open? **eon-je yeo-reo-yo?**
언제 열어요?

· What time do you
close? **eon-je da-da-yo?**
언제 닫아요?

timetable si-gan-pyo
시간표

· Where can I see the
timetable? **si-gan-pyo eo-di-seo bwa-yo?**
시간표 어디서 봐요?

· What's the timetable
for this performance? **gong-yeon si-gan-pyo-ga eo-tteo-ke doe-na-yo?**
공연 시간표가 어떻게 되나요?

The timetable is not right.

si-gan-pyo-ga dal-la-yo
시간표가 달라요.

What time is the one with the narrator?

hae-seol-sa-ga seol-myeong-hae-ju-neun geon eon-je-ye-yo?
해설사가 설명해주는 건 언제예요?

picture

sa-jin
사진

Pictures are not allowed.

sa-jin jji-geu-si-myeon an doem-ni-da
사진 찍으시면 안 됩니다.

Can I take a picture?

sa-jin jji-geo-do doe-na-yo?
사진 찍어도 되나요?

Could you take a picture?

sa-jin han jang-man jji-geo jul-lae-yo?
사진 한 장만 찍어줄래요?

Take a picture with this one.

i-geo-rang ga-chi jji-geo ju-se-yo
이거랑 같이 찍어 주세요.

· Can we take a
  picture together?

u-ri ga-chi jji-geo-do doe-na-yo?

우리 같이 찍어도 되나요?

explain

seol-myeong

설명

· Explain this, please.

i-geo seol-myeong-hae ju-se-yo

이거 설명해 주세요.

· Do you have a
  narrator?

seol-myeong-hae ju-si-neun bun i-sseo-yo?

설명해 주시는 분 있어요?

schedule

il-jeong

일정

· What's the schedule
  for this performance?

i gong-yeon seu-ke-ju-reun eon-je-ye-yo?

이 공연 스케줄은 언제예요?

· Where can I see the
  detailed schedule?

ja-se-han seu-ke-ju-reun eo-di-seo bwa-yo?

자세한 스케줄은 어디서 봐요?

| Is this schedule, right? | **i seu-ke-ju-ri ma-ja-yo?**
이 스케줄이 맞아요? |

departure

chul-bal
출발

What time is the departure?	**chul-ba-ri eon-je-ye-yo?** 출발이 언제예요?
Can we delay the departure time a little?	**chul-ba-reul jo-geum-man neut-ge ha-myeon an doe-na-yo?** 출발을 조금만 늦게 하면 안 되나요?
The departure time is too early.	**chul-bal si-ga-ni neo-mu ppal-la-yo** 출발 시간이 너무 빨라요.

arrival

do-chak
도착

| What time is the arrival? | **do-cha-gi eon-je-ye-yo?**
도착이 언제예요? |
| The arrival time is too late. | **do-chak si-ga-ni neun-ne-yo**
도착 시간이 늦네요. |

translation tong-yeok
통역

· I need a translation.　**tong-yeo-gi pi-ryo-hae-yo**
통역이 필요해요.

city tour si-ti tueo
시티 투어

· I want a city tour.　**si-ti tu-eo ha-go si-peo-yo**
시티 투어 하고 싶어요.

· I want a book for the city tour.　**si-ti tu-eo ye-ya-kal-ge-yo**
시티 투어 예약할게요.

· You got seats for the city tour?　**si-ti tu-eo ja-ri i-sseo-yo?**
시티 투어 자리 있어요?

· Only me.　**jeo hon-ja hal geo-ye-yo**
저 혼자 할 거예요.

map ji-do
지도

· You got a map?　**ji-do i-sseo-yo?**
지도 있어요?

| You got a map for the city tour? | **si-ti tu-eo ji-do i-sseo-yo?**
시티 투어 지도 있어요? |
| Could you share the map with me? | **ji-do jom ga-chi bwa-do doel-kka-yo?**
지도 좀 같이 봐도 될까요? |

gift shop seon-mul ga-ge
선물 가게

Where is the gift shop?	**seon-mul ga-ge eo-di i-sseo-yo?** 선물 가게 어디 있어요?
Is the gift shop far from here?	**seon-mul ga-ge meo-reo-yo?** 선물 가게 멀어요?
I wanna get some souvenirs.	**gi-nyeom-pum sa-ryeo-go-yo** 기념품 사려고요.

performance gong-yeon
공연

| I'm gonna see the performance. | **gong-yeon bol geo-ye-yo**
공연 볼 거예요. |

· When does the performance start?

gong-yeon eon-je si-ja-kae-yo?

공연 언제 시작해요?

· How long does the performance go on?

gong-yeon eol-ma dong-an hae-yo?

공연 얼마 동안 해요?

· The performance has been canceled.

gong-yeo-ni chwi-so-doe-eot-seum-ni-da

공연이 취소되었습니다.

reservation

ye-mae

예매

· I'd like to make a reservation.

ye-mae-ha-ryeo-go-yo

예매하려고요.

· Do I get a discount?

ha-rin-doe-na-yo?

할인되나요?

· I didn't get a reservation.

ye-mae an hae-sseo-yo

예매 안 했어요.

show time gong-yeon si-gan
공연 시간

· How long is the show time?

gong-yeon si-ga-ni eol-ma-na doe-jyo?
공연 시간이 얼마나 되죠?

· Can I eat something during the show time?

gong-yeon si-gan dong-an mwo meo-geo-do doe-na-yo?
공연 시간 동안 뭐 먹어도 되나요?

· Can I take pictures during the show time?

gong-yeon si-gan dong-an sa-jin jji-geo-do doe-na-yo?
공연 시간 동안 사진 찍어도 되나요?

· The show time is too short.

gong-yeon si-ga-ni neo-mu jjal-le-yo
공연 시간이 너무 짧네요.

· The show time is too long.

gong-yeon si-ga-ni neo-mu gi-reo-yo
공연 시간이 너무 길어요.

sold out

mae-jin
매진

Is it sold out?	**mae-jin-doe-eon-na-yo?** 매진되었나요?
What time is the next show?	**da-eum gong-yeo-neun myeot si-ye-yo?** 다음 공연은 몇 시예요?
You got no tickets at all?	**a-ye pyo-ga eop-seo-yo?** 아예 표가 없어요?
Call me when you have seats.	**ja-ri-ga na-myeon yeol-lak ju-se-yo** 자리가 나면 연락 주세요.

seat

jwa-seok
좌석

Get me a front seat.	**ap jwa-seo-geu-ro ju-se-yo** 앞 좌석으로 주세요.
Get me a back seat.	**dwit jwa-seo-geu-ro ju-se-yo** 뒷 좌석으로 주세요.

· Get me a middle seat.	jung-gan jwa-seo-geu-ro ju-se-yo 중간 좌석으로 주세요.
· Get me a good seat.	jo-eun ja-ri-ro ju-se-yo 좋은 자리로 주세요.

intermission ⊙⦻ hyu-sik si-gan
휴식 시간

· When is the intermission?	hyu-sik si-ga-ni eon-je-ye-yo? 휴식 시간이 언제예요?
· Do we get an intermission?	hyu-sik si-gan i-sseo-yo? 휴식 시간 있어요?
· How long is the intermission?	hyu-sik si-ga-ni myeot bu-ni-e-yo? 휴식 시간이 몇 분이에요?

subtitle .Smi ja-mak
자막

· You got subtitles?	ja-mak i-sseo-yo? 자막 있어요?

- You got Korean subtitles?

han-gu-geo ja-mak i-sseo-yo?
한국어 자막 있어요?

- You got English subtitles?

yeong-eo ja-mak na-wa-yo?
영어 자막 나와요?

main actor

ju-yeon-bae-u
주연배우

- Who is the main actor?

ju-yeon-bae-u-ga nu-gu-ye-yo?
주연배우가 누구예요?

- Can I meet the actors?

ju-yeon-bae-u-reul man-nal su i-sseo-yo?
주연배우를 만날 수 있어요?

- Is the main actor famous?

ju-yeon-bae-u-ga yu-myeong-hae-yo?
주연배우가 유명해요?

backstage

mu-dae
무대 뒤

· Can I go into the backstage?

mu-dae dwi-e ga-bol su in-na-yo?
무대 뒤에 가볼 수 있나요?

· You can't go into the backstage today.

o-neul-eun baek-seu-te-i-ji-e deu-reo-ga-sil su eop-seum-ni-da
오늘은 백스테이지에 들어가실 수 없습니다.

· You can take pictures with the actors at the backstage.

baek-seu-te-i-ji-e-seo bae-u-deul-gwa sa-jin-eul jji-geul su it-seum-ni-da
백스테이지에서 배우들과 사진을 찍을 수 있습니다.

No ⊘

geum-ji
금지

· No Pictures!

chwa-ryeong geum-ji
촬영 금지

· No Flash!

peul-lae-si geum-ji
플래시 금지

· No Entry!

ji-nip geum-ji
진입 금지

· No Pets!

ae-wan-dong-mul geum-ji
애완동물 금지

· No Videos!

bi-di-o chwa-ryeong geum-ji
비디오 촬영 금지

restroom | hwa-jang-sil
화장실

· Where is the restroom?

hwa-jang-sil eo-di i-sseo-yo?
화장실 어디 있어요?

· Is the restroom outside?

hwa-jang-si-reun ba-kke i-sseo-yo?
화장실은 밖에 있어요?

· Is there no restroom inside the performance hall?

hwa-jang-sil gong-yeon-jang a-ne-neun eop-seo-yo?
화장실 공연장 안에는 없어요?

Emergency situation

lost
i-reo-beo-ryeot-
sseo-yo
잃어버렸어요

quiet
jo-yong-hi hae-ju-
se-yo
조용히 해주세요

find
cha-ja-ya hae-yo
찾아야 해요

Find and speak phrases quickly!

· I lost my ticket.
ti-ket i-reo-beo-ryeo-sseo-yo
티켓 잃어버렸어요.

· I lost my bag.
ga-bang i-reo-beo-ryeo-sseo-yo
가방 잃어버렸어요.

· I lost my phone.
je hyu-dae-pon i-reo-beo-ryeo-sseo-yo
제 휴대폰 잃어버렸어요.

· I lost my friend.
je chin-gu i-reo-beo-ryeo-sseo-yo
제 친구 잃어버렸어요.

· Where is the lost and found?
bun-sil-mul sen-teo-ga eo-di-ye-yo?
분실물 센터가 어디예요?

· I gotta find my ticket.
je ti-ket cha-ja-ya hae-yo
제 티켓 찾아야 해요.

· I gotta find my friend.
je chin-gu cha-ja-ya hae-yo
제 친구 찾아야 해요.

· I gotta find my guide.
je ga-i-deu cha-ja-ya hae-yo
제 가이드 찾아야 해요.

I gotta find my bus. **je beo-seu cha-ja-ya hae-yo**
제 버스 찾아야 해요.

Can I make a call? **jeon-hwa jom sseul su i-sseo-yo?**
전화 좀 쓸 수 있어요?

I'll just make a quick call. **jeo ppal-li jeon-hwa han tong-man sseul-ge-yo**
저 빨리 전화 한 통만 쓸게요.

Please be quiet. **jo-yong-hi jom hae jwo-yo**
조용히 좀 해 줘요.

Get your phone call outside. **jeon-hwa na-ga-seo hae jwo-yo**
전화 나가서 해 줘요.

Mind your manners. **mae-neo jom ji-ki-se-yo**
매너 좀 지키세요.

When You Need Help During Your Trip to Seoul

There are tourist information centers throughout Seoul that can help if you encounter any difficulties while traveling.

In addition to providing domestic and foreign tourist information, they can help you make reservations for performances, transportation, hotels, and restaurants, and you can also obtain tourist brochures from them.

You can also get information on tourist programs in Seoul, such as the Seoul City Tour Bus and various walking tour courses.

For more information, please visit the link below.
https://korean.visitseoul.net/tourist-Information-center

When shopping

Frequently used words when shopping

01 **jeans**
cheong-ba-ji
청바지

02 **hoodie**
hu-deu
후드

03 **shirts**
syeo-cheu
셔츠

04 **skirts**
chi-ma
치마

05 **try on**
si-neo-bol-ge-yo
입어볼게요
i-beo-bol-ge-yo
신어볼게요

06 **fitting room**
pi-ting rum
피팅 룸

07 **size**
sa-i-jeu
사이즈

08 **traditional**
jeon-tong-jeo-gin geot
전통적인 것

09 **local**
ji-yeok
지역

11	**wrap**	po-jang 포장
12	**recommendation**	chu-cheon 추천
13	**gift**	seon-mul 선물
14	**pay**	ji-bul 지불
15	**discount**	ha-rin 할인
16	**sale**	se-il 세일
17	**receipt**	yeong-su-jeung 영수증
18	**browsing**	dul-leo-bo-neun geo-ye-yo 둘러보는 거예요
19	**You got?**	i-geo i-sseo-yo? 이거 있어요?

20	perfume	hyang-su
		향수
21	cosmetics	hwa-jang-pum
		화장품
22	watch	si-gye
		시계
23	bag	ga-bang
		가방
24	liquor	ju-ryu
		주류
25	fragile	kkae-ji-gi swi-wo-yo
		깨지기 쉬워요

jeans

cheong-ba-ji
청바지

· I wanna see some jeans.

cheong-ba-ji bo-ryeo-go-yo
청바지 보려고요.

· You got skinny jeans?

seu-ki-ni-jin i-sseo-yo?
스키니진 있어요?

· You got straight jeans?

il-ja cheong-ba-ji i-sseo-yo?
일자 청바지 있어요?

· You got sweatpants?

teu-re-i-ning ba-ji i-sseo-yo?
트레이닝 바지 있어요?

· You got some shorts?

ban-ba-ji i-sseo-yo?
반바지 있어요?

hoodie

hu-deu
후드

· I wanna see some hoodies.

hu-deu-ti jong-nyu bo-ryeo-go-yo
후드티 종류 보려고요.

· Where are the
hoodies?

hu-deu-ti eo-di i-sseo-yo?
후드티 어디 있어요?

· You got sweatshirts?

**teu-re-i-ning sang-ui
i-sseo-yo?**
트레이닝 상의 있어요?

shirts

syeo-cheu
셔츠

· I wanna see some
shirts.

syeo-cheu bo-ryeo-go-yo
셔츠 보려고요.

· I wanna see some
striped shirts.

**jul-mu-ni syeo-cheu bol-
ge-yo**
줄무늬 셔츠 볼게요.

· I wanna see some
dotted shirts.

**ttaeng-ttaeng-i mu-ni
syeo-cheu bol-ge-yo**
땡땡이 무늬 셔츠 볼게요.

· Is this for men?

nam-ja-yong-in-ga-yo?
남자용인가요?

· Is this for women?

yeo-ja-yong-in-ga-yo?
여자용인가요?

· You got longer ones?	**i-geot-bo-da gin syeo-cheu i-sseo-yo?** 이것보다 긴 셔츠 있어요?
· I also wanna see some ties.	**nek-ta-i-do bol geo-ye-yo** 넥타이도 볼 거예요.

skirts

chi-ma
치마

· I wanna see some skirts.	**chi-ma bo-ryeo-go-yo** 치마 보려고요.
· You got long skirts?	**gin chi-ma i-sseo-yo?** 긴 치마 있어요?
· You got short skirts?	**jjal-beun chi-ma i-sseo-yo?** 짧은 치마 있어요?
· You got dresses?	**deu-re-seu i-sseo-yo?** 드레스 있어요?

try on

i-beo-bol-ge-yo/
si-neo-bol-ge-yo
입어볼게요/신어볼게요

· I wanna try this on.	**i-geo i-beo-bol-ge-yo** 이거 입어볼게요.
· I wanna try this on.	**i-geo si-neo-bol-ge-yo** 이거 신어볼게요.
· I wanna try another one.	**da-reun geo i-beo-bol-ge-yo** 다른 거 입어볼게요.
· I wanna try another size.	**da-reun sa-i-jeu si-neo-bol-ge-yo** 다른 사이즈 신어볼게요.

fitting room

pi-ting rum
피팅 룸

· Where is the fitting room?	**pi-ting rum eo-di-ye-yo?** 피팅 룸 어디예요?
· I can't find the fitting room.	**pi-ting rum mot chat-ge-sseo-yo** 피팅 룸 못 찾겠어요.

· How many can I try on?	**myeot gae i-beo-bol su i-sseo-yo?** 몇 개 입어볼 수 있어요?
· I didn't try this one.	**i-geon an i-beo bwa-sseo-yo** 이건 안 입어 봤어요.
· I'm gonna buy this one.	**i-geo sal geo-ye-yo** 이거 살 거예요.

size   sai-jeu
사이즈

· What size do you wear?	**sa-i-jeu-ga eo-tteo-ke doe-se-yo?** 사이즈가 어떻게 되세요?
· It's too big.	**keo-yo** 커요.
· It's too small.	**ja-ga-yo** 작아요.
· I want a bigger size.	**deo keun geol-lo ju-se-yo** 더 큰 걸로 주세요.
· I want a smaller size.	**deo ja-geun geol-lo ju-se-yo** 더 작은 걸로 주세요.

traditional

jeon-tong-jeo-gin geot
전통적인 것

· You got something traditional?

jeon-tong-jeo-gin mul-geon i-sseo-yo?
전통적인 물건 있어요?

· You got something traditional to eat?

jeon-tong-jeo-gin eum-sik i-sseo-yo?
전통적인 음식 있어요?

· Which one do you think is the best to get as a gift?

yeo-gi-seo seon-mul-ha-gi jo-eun ge mwo-ye-yo?
여기서 선물하기 좋은 게 뭐예요?

local

ji-yeok
지역

· What's the most famous local thing here?

i ji-yeo-ge-seo yu-myeong-han ge mwo-ye-yo?
이 지역에서 유명한 게 뭐예요?

· You got famous local products?

ji-yeok teuk-san-pum i-sseo-yo?
지역 특산품 있어요?

· Which one do you think is the best to get as a gift?

yeo-gi-e-seo seon-mul-ha-gi jo-eun ge mwo-ye-yo?

여기서 선물하기 좋은 게 뭐예요?

wrap 🎁

po-jang

포장

· Wrap this as a gift, please.

po-jang-hae ju-se-yo

포장해 주세요.

· Only this one goes as a gift.

po-jang-eun i-geo ha-na-man hae ju-se-yo

포장은 이거 하나만 해 주세요.

· Do I need to pay an extra charge?

po-jang-ha-neun de don deu-reo-yo?

포장하는 데 돈 들어요?

· It's too expensive.

neo-mu bi-ssa-yo

너무 비싸요.

· I'll just wrap it up myself at home.

geu-nyang nae-ga ji-be-seo po-jang-hal-ge-yo

그냥 내가 집에서 포장할게요.

249

recommendation

· Any
recommendations?

**chu-cheon-hal man-han
ot i-sseo-yo?**
추천할 만한 옷 있어요?

· Any recommendation
for gifts?

**chu-cheon-hal man-han
seon-mul i-sseo-yo?**
추천할 만한 선물 있어요?

· Recommend a gift
for my parents,
please.

**bu-mo-nim seon-mul chu-
cheon-hae ju-se-yo**
부모님 선물 추천해 주세요.

· Recommend a gift
for my boyfriend,
please.

**nam-ja-chin-gu seon-mul
chu-cheon-hae ju-se-yo**
남자친구 선물 추천해 주세요.

· Recommend a gift
for my girlfriend,
please.

**yeo-ja-chin-gu seon-mul
chu-cheon-hae ju-se-yo**
여자친구 선물 추천해 주세요.

· Please recommend
something that goes
well with this.

**i o-si-rang eo-ul-lil-man-
han geol-lo chu-cheon
jom hae ju-se-yo**
이 옷이랑 어울릴만한 걸로 추천 좀 해 주세
요.

gift

seon-mul

선물

- It's a gift.

seon-mul-lo ju-ryeo-go-yo

선물로 주려고요.

- Get this one wrapped up as a gift.

seon-mul po-jang-hae ju-se-yo

선물 포장해 주세요.

- What's good as a gift?

seon-mul-lo mwo-ga jo-eun-ga-yo?

선물로 뭐가 좋은가요?

- How about this as a gift?

i-geo seon-mul-lo eo-ttae-yo?

이거 선물로 어때요?

Pay

ji-bul

지불

- How would you like to pay?

ji-bu-reun eo-tteo-ke ha-si-ge-sseo-yo?

지불은 어떻게 하시겠어요?

- Do you take credit cards?

sin-yong-ka-deu doe-na-yo?

신용카드 되나요?

· I'll pay in cash.

hyeon-geu-meu-ro hal-ge-yo
현금으로 할게요.

discount

ha-rin
할인

· Can I get a discount?

ha-rin-doe-na-yo?
할인되나요?

· I have a discount coupon.

ha-rin ku-pon i-sseo-yo
할인 쿠폰 있어요.

sale

se-il
세일

· Is this on sale?

i-geo se-il-hae-yo?
이거 세일해요?

· Is this the sale price?

i-geo se-il geu-mae-gi-e-yo?
이거 세일 금액이에요?

· This one is not on sale.

i-geon se-il pum-mo-gi a-nim-ni-da
이건 세일 품목이 아닙니다.

receipt 🧾

yeong-su-jeung
영수증

· You want the
receipt?

yeong-su-jeung deu-ril-kka-yo?
영수증 드릴까요?

· I want the receipt.

yeong-su-jeung ju-se-yo
영수증 주세요.

· You didn't give me
the receipt.

yeong-su-jeung an ju-syeo-sseo-yo
영수증 안 주셨어요.

· I need the receipt.

yeong-su-jeung pi-ryo-hae-yo
영수증 필요해요.

browsing 😮

dul-leo-bo-neun geo-ye-yo
둘러보는 거예요.

· I'm just browsing.

geu-nyang bo-neun geo-ye-yo
그냥 보는 거예요.

· I'll just look around
by myself.

hon-ja dul-leo bol-ge-yo
혼자 둘러 볼게요.

· I'll call you when I
need you. Thank you.
**do-u-mi pi-ryo-ha-myeon
bu-reul-ge-yo. gam-sa-
hae-yo**
도움이 필요하면 부를게요. 감사해요.

You got?

i-geo i-sseo-yo?
이거 있어요?

· You got another one?
da-reun geo i-sseo-yo?
다른 거 있어요?

· You got another
color?
**saek-kkal da-reun geo
i-sseo-yo?**
색깔 다른 거 있어요?

· You got bigger ones?
keun geo i-sseo-yo?
큰 거 있어요?

· You got smaller
ones?
ja-geun geo i-sseo-yo?
작은 거 있어요?

· You got this same
one that's not
displayed?
**jin-yeol an doe-eo it-deon
geo i-sseo-yo?**
진열 안 되어 있던 거 있어요?

perfume

hyang-su
향수

· I wanna see some perfume.

hyang-su bo-ryeo-go-yo
향수 보려고요.

· I wanna try this one.

i-geo si-hyang-hae bol-ge-yo
이거 시향해 볼게요.

· You got sweet fragrance?

dal-kom-han hyang i-sseo-yo?
달콤한 향 있어요?

· You got fresh fragrance?

sang-keum-han hyang i-sseo-yo?
상큼한 향 있어요?

cosmetics

hwa-jang-pum
화장품

· I wanna see some cosmetics.

hwa-jang-pum bo-ryeo-go-yo
화장품 보려고요.

· Where are the cosmetics?	**hwa-jang-pum ko-neo eo-di-ye-yo?** 화장품 코너 어디예요?
· Show me some creams.	**keu-rim bo-yeo-ju-se-yo** 크림 보여주세요.
· Show me some lipsticks.	**rip-seu-tik bo-yeo-ju-se-yo** 립스틱 보여주세요.
· Show me some foundations.	**pa-un-de-i-syeon bo-yeo-ju-se-yo** 파운데이션 보여주세요.
· Show me some mascaras.	**ma-seu-ka-ra bo-yeo-ju-se-yo** 마스카라 보여주세요.

watch

si-gye
시계

· I wanna see some watches.	**son-mok-si-gye bo-ryeo-go-yo** 손목시계 보려고요.
· Show me some watches for women.	**yeo-ja si-gye-ro bo-yeo-ju-se-yo** 여자 시계로 보여주세요.

· Show me some watches for men.

nam-ja si-gye-ro bo-yeo-ju-se-yo
남자 시계로 보여주세요.

· Show me some watches for kids.

eo-ri-ni si-gye-ro bo-yeo-ju-se-yo
어린이 시계로 보여주세요.

bag

ga-bang
가방

· I wanna to see some bags.

ga-bang bo-ryeo-go-yo
가방 보려고요.

· Show me some shoulder bags.

syol-deo-baek bo-yeo-ju-se-yo
숄더백 보여주세요.

· Show me some tote bags.

to-teu-baek bo-yeo-ju-se-yo
토트백 보여주세요.

· Show me some clutch bags.

keul-leo-chi bo-yeo-ju-se-yo
클러치 보여주세요.

· Show me some wallets.

ji-gap bo-yeo-ju-se-yo
지갑 보여주세요.

· Show me wallets for men.	**nam-ja ji-gap bo-yeo-ju-se-yo** 남자 지갑 보여주세요.
· Show me wallets for women.	**yeo-ja ji-gap bo-yeo-ju-se-yo** 여자 지갑 보여주세요.

liquor 🍷

주류

· Where do I get liquor?	**ju-ryu-neun eo-di-seo sa-yo?** 주류는 어디서 사요?
· Show me some whisky.	**wi-seu-ki bo-yeo-ju-se-yo** 위스키 보여주세요.
· Show me some Valentine.	**bal-len-ta-in bo-yeo-ju-se-yo** 발렌타인 보여주세요.
· Show me some wine.	**wa-in bo-yeo-ju-se-yo** 와인 보여주세요.
· How many bottles can I get?	**je-ga myeot byeong sal su i-sseo-yo?** 제가 몇 병살 수 있어요?

fragile ♛   kkae-ji-gi swi-wo-yo
깨지기 쉬워요.

· This is fragile.   **i-geo kkae-ji-gi swi-wo-yo**
이거 깨지기 쉬워요.

· Be cautious.   **jo-sim-ha-syeo-ya hae-yo**
조심하셔야 해요.

· Please wrap it well.   **jal po-jang-hae ju-se-yo**
잘 포장해 주세요.

Emergency situation

have paid
don nae-sseo-yo
돈 냈어요!

exchange
gyo-hwan
교환

refund
hwan-bul
환불

already
i-mi
이미

too small
neo-mu ja-ga-yo
너무 작아요

too big
neo-mu keo-yo
너무 커요

doesn't fit
an ma-ja-yo
안 맞아요

Find and speak phrases quickly!

· I have paid!

i-mi don nae-sseo-yo!
이미 돈 냈어요!

· It's not fair.

gong-pyeong-ha-ji an-ne-yo
공평하지 않네요.

· Call the police.

gyeong-cha-reul bul-leo-jwo-yo
경찰을 불러줘요.

· I wanna call the embassy.

dae-sa-gwa-ne jeon-hwa-ha-ge-sseo-yo
대사관에 전화하겠어요.

· Call a translator.

tong-yeo-geul bul-leo-yo
통역을 불러요.

· I wanna exchange this.

gyo-hwan-ha-go si-peo-yo
교환하고 싶어요.

· Do you have your receipt?

yeong-su-jeung i-sseu-se-yo?
영수증 있으세요?

· Why do you want an exchange?

wae gyo-hwan-ha-si-ryeo-go-yo?
왜 교환하시려고요?

What would you like to exchange this for?	eo-tteon geol-lo gyo-hwan-ha-si-ge-sseo-yo? 어떤 걸로 교환하시겠어요?
It's not working.	go-jang-na-sseo-yo 고장났어요.
I don't like it.	ma-eu-me an deu-reo-yo 마음에 안 들어요.
Because of the size.	sa-i-jeu ttae-mu-ne-yo 사이즈 때문에요.
I wanna refund this.	i-geo hwan-bul-ha-go si-peo-yo 이거 환불하고 싶어요.
Do you have your receipt?	yeong-su-jeung i-sseu-se-yo? 영수증 있으세요?
Why do you want a refund?	wae hwan-bul-ha-si-ryeo-go ha-se-yo? 왜 환불하시려고 하세요?
Do you have your credit card?	(gyeol-je-ha-syeot-deon) ka-deu i-sseu-se-yo? (결제하셨던) 카드 있으세요?

· I've already opened the package.	**i-mi po-jang-eul tteut-gin hae-sseo-yo** 이미 포장을 뜯긴 했어요.
· But I didn't used it.	**geun-de an sseo-sseo-yo** 근데 안 썼어요.
· Check it again.	**da-si han-beon hwa-gin-ha-se-yo** 다시 한번 확인하세요.
· It's too small.	**neo-mu ja-ga-yo** 너무 작아요.
· I want a smaller one.	**ja-geun geol-lo ba-kkwo ju-se-yo** 작은 걸로 바꿔 주세요.
· It's too big.	**neo-mu keo-yo** 너무 커요.
· I want a bigger one.	**keun geol-lo ba-kkwo ju-se-yo** 큰 걸로 바꿔 주세요.
· It doesn't fit.	**i-geo an ma-ja-yo** 이거 안 맞아요.
· I want another one.	**da-reun geol-lo ju-se-yo** 다른 걸로 주세요.

memo

Top 8 Street Foods in Myeongdong

Dalgona

Egg bread

Deep-fried and Braised chicken

Sotteok sotteok

Eomuk

Fish-shaped bun

Chicken Skewers

Hotteok

When returning home

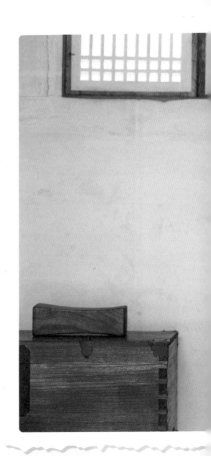

Frequently used words when returning home

01 confirm — hwa-gin
확인

02 change — byeon-gyeong
변경

03 delay — yeon-chak
연착

04 request — yo-cheong
요청

05 transit — hwan-seung
환승

06 return — ban-nap
반납

07 limit — je-han
제한

Find and speak phrases quickly!

confirm   **hwa-gin**
확인

· I wanna confirm my flight.

je bi-haeng-gi hwa-gin-ha-ryeo-go-yo
제 비행기 확인하려고요.

· I wanna confirm my ticket.

je ti-ket hwa-gin-ha-ryeo-go-yo
제 티켓 확인하려고요.

· I wanna confirm my seat.

je ja-ri hwa-gin-ha-ryeo-go-yo
제 자리 확인하려고요.

change   **byeon-gyeong**
변경

· I wanna change my flight.

je bi-haeng-gi byeon-gyeong-ha-ryeo-go-yo
제 비행기 변경하려고요.

· I wanna change my ticket.

je ti-ket byeon-gyeong-ha-ryeo-go-yo
제 티켓 변경하려고요.

· I wanna change my
seat.

**je ja-ri byeon-gyeong-ha-
ryeo-go-yo**
제 자리 변경하려고요.

delay   yeon-chak
연착

· The flight was
delayed.

**bi-haeng-gi-ga yeon-
chak-doe-eot-seum-ni-da**
비행기가 연착되었습니다.

· How long do I wait?

eol-ma-na gi-da-ryeo-yo?
얼마나 기다려요?

· Can I change my
flight?

**da-reun bi-haeng-gi-ro
ba-kkul su i-sseo-yo?**
다른 비행기로 바꿀 수 있어요?

request 🗣   yo-cheong
요청

· I wanna request a
vegetarian meal.

**gi-nae-si-geul chae-si-
geu-ro yo-cheoung-ha-
ryeo-go-yo**
기내식을 채식으로 요청하려고요.

· I wanna request a kids' meal.	**eo-ri-ni gi-nae-si-geu-ro yo-cheong-ha-ryeo-go-yo** 어린이 기내식으로 요청하려고요.
· I didn't request in advance.	**mi-ri yo-cheong-eun an hae-sseo-yo** 미리 요청은 안 했어요.
· Is it impossible to request now?	**ji-geum yo-cheong-i bul-ga-neung-hae-yo?** 지금 요청이 불가능해요?
· Come on, cut me some slack.	**jom hae jwo-yo** 좀 해 줘요.

transit

hwan-seung

환승

· I'm a transit passenger.	**jeo hwan-seung seung-gae-gin-de-yo** 저 환승 승객인데요.
· Where is a transit lounge?	**hwan-seung ra-un-ji-neun eo-di-ye-yo?** 환승 라운지는 어디예요?

- I'm a transit passenger to New York.

gyeong-yu-hae-seo nyu-yo-geu-ro gal geo-ye-yo
경유해서 뉴욕으로 가요.

return

ban-nap
반납

- I wanna return the phone.

hyu-dae-pon ban-na-pa-ryeo-go-yo
휴대폰 반납하려고요.

- I wanna return the car.

ren-teu-ka ban-na-pa-ryeo-go-yo
렌트카 반납하려고요.

limit

je-han
제한

- How much is the weight limit?

jung-nyang je-ha-ni eol-ma-ye-yo?
중량 제한이 얼마예요?

- How about the limit on board?

gi-nae jung-nyang je-han-eun-yo?
기내 중량 제한은요?

Emergency situation

lost

i-reo-beo-ryeo-
sseo-yo
잃어버렸어요

miss

no-chyeo-sseo-yo
놓쳤어요

next flight

da-eum bi-haeng-
pyeon
다음 비행편

Find and speak phrases quickly!

I lost my boarding pass.
je hang-gong-gwo-neul i-reo-beo-ryeo-sseo-yo
제 항공권을 잃어버렸어요.

I lost my passport.
je yeo-gwo-neul i-reo-beo-ryeo-sseo-yo
제 여권을 잃어버렸어요.

I lost my baggage tag.
je su-hwa-mul-pyo-reul i-reo-beo-ryeo-sseo-yo
제 수하물표를 잃어버렸어요.

I missed my flight.
bi-haeng-gi-reul no-chyeo-sseo-yo
비행기를 놓쳤어요.

I missed my flight, who do I ask?
bi-haeng-gi-reul no-chyeon-neun-de nu-gu-han-te mu-reo-bwa-yo?
비행기를 놓쳤는데 누구한테 물어봐요?

When is the next flight?
da-eum bi-haeng-pyeo-neun eon-je-ye-yo?
다음 비행편은 언제예요?

What should I do?
jeon eo-tteo-ka-na-yo?
전 어떡하나요?

· I'm okay with a different airline.

da-reun hang-gong-sa-do sang-gwan-eop-seo-yo

다른 항공사도 상관없어요.

· How much extra do you charge?

eol-ma-na chu-ga-yo- geu-mi bun-neun-de-yo?

얼마나 추가요금이 붙는데요?

memo

Have Fun in Korea

Yeouido Fireworks Festival

N Seoul tower

Gyeongbokgung palace

Dongdaemun Design Plaza(DDP)

Korean airplane

The night view of Seoul

The Byeolmadang Library

Gyeongbokgung Palace

Gamcheon Culture Village

DDP (Dongdaemun Design Plaza)

Korean diner

Gyeongbokgung Palace

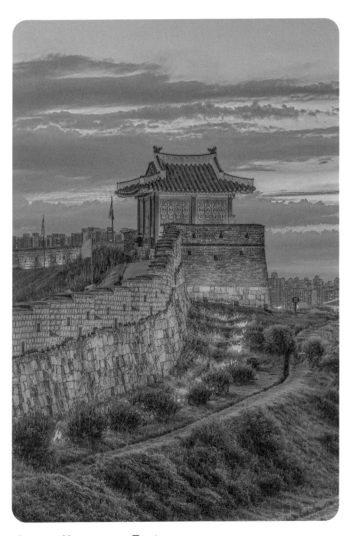

Suwon Hwaseong Fortres

Korean guesthouse

SIWONSCHOOL
——— KOREAN